FiNDING
A VOICE

D1428624

First published in 2011 by
Darton, Longman and Todd Ltd
1 Spencer Court
140–142 Wandsworth High Street
London SW18 4JJ

© 2011 Hilary Brand

The right of Hilary Brand to be identified as the Author
of this work has been asserted in accordance with the
Copyright, Designs and Patents Act 1998.

ISBN 978-0-232-52893-0

A catalogue record for this book is available from the British Library.

Designed and produced by Judy Linard

Printed and bound by
CPI Group (UK) Ltd, Croydon, CR0 4YY

CONTENTS

♔
INTRODUCTION

Over the centuries Lent has lost its radical edge. For most people now it is a residual custom involving the brief forswearing of chocolate or booze, and perhaps in some church quarters getting together in groups to chat about religious stuff – in these strange things we call Lent courses.

It was intended to be much more. Historically, Lent was a time for strengthening and for preparation: a time when fasting strengthened flagging will-power; when prayer and meditation prepared for Easter when baptismal vows were renewed. It was based on Christ's forty days in the wilderness. Just as Jesus knew how vital was that strengthening and preparation for what was to come, so it seems did his early followers. In those tough times, they understood, rather more than we do, what a radical and crucial calling they had to fulfil.

FULFILLING POTENTIAL

Followers of Jesus Christ are described in the New Testament as 'a royal priesthood'[1] and as the recipients of a 'glorious inheritance' and an 'incomparably great power'[2] – people with incredible potential and enormous responsibility; people with a duty – to speak with authority about that which is loving and true.

Yet these days many of us seem to have lost our voice. So eloquent are the voices raised against faith – and often so subtly dismissive – that we no longer believe we have a right to be heard. So private has our religion become that propriety prevents us either revealing our pain or offering encouragement. So flabby are our wills and so strong are our fears that we have lost the sense of who we could become and what together we might accomplish.

That is why Lent remains important and why Lent courses, if entered into with honesty and commitment, can be vital staging posts in the journey towards fulfilling spiritual potential. And why, in this case, a film like *The King's Speech* is such a powerful tool.

When I first saw the film I immediately realised how many of its strands resonated with the teaching of the Bible. The Old Testament is full of tongue-tied and terrified leaders; the New Testament is full of commands to encourage one another. Both Jesus and the apostles had strong messages about the power of words for good and for evil. Both Old and New Testaments are full of the idea being called to a task – and often that calling is to speak out. Beneath all that is the amazing promise of the Holy Spirit as an encourager, standing at our side, unseen by the wider world – a concept I saw as given a memorable image in the character of Lionel Logue.

FICTION AND REALITY

This film, of course, is about real events and real people, including our own Queen still alive today. Many course participants may have read biographical material about the characters, and some may even remember the events in question! It is important therefore to make it clear that for the purposes of simplicity and clarity, this Lent course is based almost entirely on the *film*, which is obviously very much a *fictionalised* account. The events covered are actually spread over a time span of 14 years, and while the film does flag this up in giving dates, the overall impression is inevitably that these things are happening much more closely together than they really did. (The fact that the princesses do not age during this time is also obviously somewhat misleading!)

In point of fact, Bertie would have had to do live Christmas broadcasts from the time he became King, so the speech at the outbreak of war might not have been the major trial it appears, rather a culminating point of many such trials. The film chooses what to the King may have been just one moment in a long process, and condenses it for dramatic effect.

In reality, from the point at which he became King, Bertie's whole life would have been one long slog of speeches – opening hospitals, launching ships, attending dinners, entertaining dignitaries – week in, week out, year in year out. Understanding the sheer courage and nervous energy that must have entailed makes the fact far more heroic than the fiction. But without the fiction would most of us really have understood?

If you watch newsreel footage of King George VI making a speech you will hear many uncomfortable pauses – and clearly the most uncomfortable of them have been edited out – but so controlled was he that you rarely hear the stutter. You do not hear the excruciating attempts of the mouth to form the words, you do not see the terror in the eyes, you cannot sense the agonising struggle of the mind. A historian could tell you those things were there, a newsreel could give evidence and you might well accept it as fact. A movie makes you *feel* it – joins head and heart in understanding the truth of it – and therein lies its strength.

The strength of this particular film is that it was written with such integrity by a man who really knew the feeling of being imprisoned by a stammer. Screenwriter David Seidler understood all too well what it was to 'live in self-imposed silence because it is too painful to speak'.[3]

Seidler, as a small child in wartime, had heard the King on the radio and been inspired by his courage. As he grew up, he too learned all the tricks to cover his stammer. Nevertheless the childhood emotions remained. It was not until the age of 73 when the film became such a hit, that he felt a freedom he had never had before. It was at a gala showing of the film in Toronto where the entire audience stood to applaud, that, he recalls: 'For the first time ever the penny dropped and I felt I had a voice and had been heard. For a stutterer, that's a profound moment.'[4]

The reason why this success was so late-blooming is also evidence of Seidler's integrity. In the early 1980s he wrote to the Queen Mother asking her for permission to use Logue's notebooks as a basis for his screenplay. She wrote back saying, 'Please, Mr Seidler, not during my lifetime, the memory of those events is still too painful.'[5] And although he did not need to, he dutifully complied. He was not to know that she would live for another 20 years! But out of respect he waited – and waited. And he tried in that time to do his research and make the outcome as historically accurate as possible.

Of course, as he points out, untidy and unpredictable real life does not always fit within the constraints of drama.

> People, even kings, don't always have the good grace to live their lives in an orderly three-act structure. But I tried as best I could to get to the truth, at least the inner truth.[6]

The fact that such a relatively low-budget film on such an obscure subject has swept the board at the awards ceremonies and continues to be such a popular work, testifies that he did so.

Speaking at the BAFTA awards, Helena Bonham-Carter pointed out that it was not just about overcoming a stammer, but about gaining self-esteem. Colin Firth said that it was about the journey not just towards becoming a King, but to becoming a human being.

It is about a journey we all tread. In Bertie we see our own anxieties played out. In Logue we glimpse our own disappointments. In King George V, we see those who have discouraged us and in David, Prince of Wales, those who have scorned us. But we also see other things we know to be true: the power of perseverance, of courage and above all of friendship.

C.S. Lewis in one of his wartime letters wrote, 'Is any pleasure on earth as great as a circle of Christian friends by a fire?'[7] I don't know whether there will be a fireside in your

Lenten gathering, but whether you meet around a flickering hearth or in a draughty church hall, whether you come together as long-term colleagues or as strangers on a journey, I pray that out of this course will come for you real friendship and lots of pleasure.

HOW THE COURSE WORKS

This book offers five weekly group sessions each with two accompanying chapters, to be read individually, before and after the session. Each group session is timed to be about an hour and a half long (but could easily stretch to two hours). Each includes two clips from *The Kings Speech*. It is possible to follow the course without having seen the film through beforehand, but it is not advisable. Many of you may have seen the film some time ago and think you know it. You probably won't remember anything like as much as you think! So please, if you possibly can, make a point of seeing the film right through before the course starts. Hopefully, this is something that group leaders will arrange.

At the end of the course is a suggestion for a sixth session, which I hope will be entertaining but also provide a practical challenge to help in this business of finding a voice.

This course covers some tough subjects: fear, discouragement, bad language; ones in which participants may have raw feelings or strong opinions. It is essential then, right at the beginning, to approach group sessions with respect and sensitivity towards each other. This is not to say that such subjects should be tiptoed around. The whole point of this course is that it allows people to be totally honest and to talk about issues often avoided. Rather it means that others in the group need to be accepted for who they are and where they are, that differences need to be embraced and diversity valued as the great teacher it so often can be.

Suggested ground rules for group sessions

- Give space for every member of the group who wishes to speak to do so.
- Speak as much as possible from your experience, rather than at a theoretical level.
- Actively listen to each contribution, rather than thinking about what you would like to say.
- Respect each other's viewpoints and if possible, try and understand what formed them.
- Make it a rule that nothing said within the group is repeated outside. Make it a safe place to be honest.

WEEK 1

'I'm trying to get you to realise
you need not be governed by fear.'

♔

TO START YOU THINKING

God's opening gambit

'Do not be afraid, Abram. I am your shield.' (Genesis 15:1)

Read
Genesis 15:1-6

Should you happen to have time on your hands one day, a trawl through the Old Testament can be very instructive. You will discover a fair amount of blood and bludgeoning, a great deal of dodgy tribal ethics, a few salacious bits they never told you in Sunday School, and a bizarre mix of flawed protagonists that may well leave you asking God, 'Whatever were you thinking of?'

You may also discover that whenever God has a conversation with one of these dubious heroes, his opening gambit is nearly always the same: 'Do not be afraid.'

Hardly surprising, you might think. If you came face to face with the Almighty or one of his ministering angels, you too might feel a little unnerved. But almost always God is coming right to the heart of these guys' problems. He knows exactly where their fear is rooted.

In the case of Abram (later to be known as Abraham, the father of the Jewish people) it was his virility that was in question – a pretty deep male fear, that one. Abram had built himself up to become a tribal leader to be reckoned with. In an era when wealth was evaluated in sheep, oxen and donkeys, he was approaching millionaire status. But despite a series of promises from God that he would be the father of a great nation, he had not one child to inherit it all. Maybe his habit of passing his wife off as his sister and offering her favours to neighbouring kings had something to do with it. One wonders what sexually-transmitted diseases were around in those days, and whether that might have been a factor. (See Genesis 12:10-20 and 20:1-18, if you really want to know) Why was he doing that? Well, out of fear, obviously. Given Sarah's evident desirability and the propensity of tribal despots to get what they wanted by any means, it was a rather cowardly way of keeping his head attached to his body.

Whatever we may think of it, God did work with Abram, despite his flaws and despite his fears, and the promise of a son was fulfilled. Again and again, throughout Old Testament and New, God takes some very unlikely candidates, deals with their fears, and turns them into great leaders. It seems to be the divine stock-in-trade.

Which is why, I suppose, when I first saw *The King's Speech* I immediately felt a spiritual resonance.

The Hollywood machine spends billions of dollars turning out scary movies, creating better and better special effects in the hope of eliciting that vicarious thrill that is so successful in putting certain sorts of bums on seats. Yet if there has ever been a greater cinematic portrayal of fear than the opening sequence of *The King's Speech*, I can't recall it. It is the stuff of nightmares – suddenly finding yourself completely tongue-tied and unprepared, called upon to speak in front of millions of people.

My husband can certainly identify with this. He spent most of his career in BBC radio, beginning as a sound operator for the World Service. On nightshifts, as a nervous 19-year-old trainee, part of his duty was to do the service announcements between programmes. Throughout his life, if he has a nightmare, it is always of the red light suddenly coming on and not knowing what to say.

I too can identify: I was so shy that it took me until I was 40 years old to have the courage to express my views in a large group or a classroom situation, let alone stand up and speak before an audience. I can do it now, though I'm not sure what triggered the change. Interesting though, that it was about that time that I wrote the little fable reproduced on p. 41: *The prince who forgot who he was*. Maybe that was part of me working it through.

And maybe that is why, as I have put together this course, I have kept returning to a certain sentence in the New Testament, from one of the apostle Peter's letters:

> You are a chosen people, a royal priesthood, a holy nation, a people belonging to God, that you may declare the praises of him who called you out of darkness into his wonderful light. (1 Peter 2: 9)

I know that this idea of a chosen people, with its racist connotations and accompanying doctrine of predestination, can cause more problems than it solves, creating dangerous and divisive ideas of elitism and favouritism.

That is not how I understand it. Rather I would say that God picks up on even the smallest longing in the human heart: to be better, to be loving, to be moral, and says 'Ah, now that's someone I can work with'. In fact, this is one of Christianity's many paradoxes: if you think you've made it, you haven't; if you think you're at the top of the heap, you aren't. If you are not afraid in one way or another, if you are not aware of your own flaws and weaknesses, then perhaps you are not malleable enough to be used.

But ultimately fear needs to be dealt with. It will always entrap us and hold us back unless it is managed. Philosopher Nicolas Berdyaev said that:

> Victory over fear is the first spiritual duty of man.[1]

For Berdyaev, writing in Russia in the early twentieth century, such a victory came at a cost. Berdyaev believed in both radical socialism and Christianity, but could not accept the oppressive power of either the Orthodox Church or the Bolsheviks. For him, fulfilling his spiritual duty and speaking out led to 26 years in exile.

The King's Speech too demonstrates how costly this victory can be. It demands courage, perseverance and the will to succeed. But as the film shows, what really makes the difference is not going it alone. It is often said that the opposite of love is fear, and it seems it works both ways. 'Perfect love drives out fear', says the apostle John.[2] The Christian writer John Gunstone expands on it thus:

> The best answer to fear is to have a firm grasp of what it means to be accepted by God.[3]

So as you begin this Lenten study, take to yourself God's oft-repeated command, 'Do not be afraid.' Because it comes with a promise:

　'I am your shield.'

Lord of my Lenten journey,
Who calls me, flawed and fearful as I am,
I acknowledge before you now my mixed feelings:
*　　wanting to be loving one minute*
*　　　not being bothered the next;*
*　　wanting to move forward one day,*
*　　　wanting to be undisturbed the next.*
I bring before you now the fears, acknowledged and
unrecognised, that hold me back.
I invite your love to do its work.
Take me as I am. Do with me as you will.
Amen.

SESSION 1

The stuff of nightmares and the power of friendship

Introductions   *10-15 mins*
(As appropriate for participants)

We bring to this Lent course a wide variety of experiences, different views of faith and discipleship, varying doubts and struggles, priorities and opinions – but if we come as followers of Jesus Christ, then, according to the apostle Peter, we have one very surprising thing in common. In God's eyes we are all royalty!

Read   *2 mins*
I Peter 2 v9

> 'You are a chosen race, a royal priesthood, a holy nation, God's own people – in order that you might proclaim the mighty acts of him who called you out of darkness into his wonderful light.'

And then read through again slowly.

We will return to that passage in a later session, but for now, as we begin this course, just take with you these three basic messages from that remarkable verse:

- You are very special to God
- He has called you from a place of darkness to a place of light (and if you haven't taken that step yet, he is inviting you to do so)
- He has called you to 'proclaim' – somehow in your life to make it clear and explicit: who you follow, why you do so and what that means for you and your world.

With that as a background, let's turn to the film. As it starts we meet a royal prince, Bertie, Prince Albert, Duke of York, second in line to the throne. But we meet him first as an ordinary man, in commoner's clothes, in a dingy corridor – and at this moment terrified out of his wits.

Show   *7 mins*
(Chapter 1) Bertie addressing the crowd at Wembley.

Brainstorm   *4 mins*
What do you thing are the fears inside Bertie's head as he waits to take the podium? List as many possibilities as you can think of.

We have just seen Bertie living through his worst nightmare – standing in front of a vast crowd and the words just refusing to come out. And then to make things worse he faces another nightmare – humiliating treatment by a so-called expert and the fear of choking on marbles.

Discuss   *6 mins*
Do you have any recurring nightmares? If so what are they?

Ponder and share   *6 mins*
What is your worst 'social' fear?

(N.B. Not the spiders or heights or hypodermic needle type of fears, but those things you fear most in relationships with others or in social situations.)
    If you don't have any 'social' fears – has that always been the case? If not, how did you overcome them?

Ask   *3 mins*
As Bertie goes up to the podium, what things are flagged up in the opening sequence that make the ordeal even more terrifying for him?

Discuss   *5 mins*

Bertie is facing not just his own attempts to make a speech, but the incredibly high expectations of others. In which areas of life do you not attempt something you might otherwise try, because of fear that you won't to live up to the high standards others impose on you?

Fear, it seems is a universal part of the human condition. We all understand the sort of fear that aids our safety: not going too near the bonfire or the edge of the cliff. But what about the problem of 'social' fear?

Read   *2 mins*
Jeremiah 1:4-10

Discuss   *3 mins*
What possible reason might there be for God choosing someone who 'cannot speak' to act as his spokesman?

Discuss   *3 mins*
Can you think of any occasions when fear can be useful? (Again looking at 'social' fear, rather than the not-touching-fire, edge-of-a-cliff sort of situations)

Ask   *1 min*
What are the two 'do not's in that passage?

Ponder and share   *4 mins*
Have you ever excused yourself from action or speech with '*I am only....*'?
    If so, '*I am only ...*' what?

One of the hardest things is to stand alone and speak out alone. It seems that this is what God called Jeremiah to do – and that he rose to the challenge. But most of us don't have the strength to go it alone, and thankfully the New Testament paints a different picture. But before we turn to that picture, we return to the film, and jump to almost the end of the story.

Bertie has been made King and now war has been declared against Germany. Bertie faces the biggest challenge of his life – a live broadcast with little time to prepare, and the task of inspiring the nation with courage in this difficult hour.

Show 5 *mins*

(Chapter 11) The King's wartime speech.

Ask 2 *min*

Bertie's stutter has not disappeared, but what makes all the difference in helping him rise to this challenge?

Ask 1 *min*

Besides Lionel Logue, the speech therapist, who else stands with him at this time, and how do they encourage him?

Ask 1 *min*

What did you notice on the faces of those ordinary people who were listening to the broadcast?

Read 2 *min*

1 John 4:7-21

Ask 1 *min*

What key phrase reveals the antidote to 'social' fear?

Discuss 3 *mins*

Is it our love for others that conquers fear, or others' love for us? Can you have one without the other? And which comes first?

MEDITATION 6 *mins*

Leader

The traditional purpose of Lent is to seek to become better followers of Jesus Christ. Let us return to the verse we began with and remind ourselves of the incredible privilege and responsibility of being one of those followers:

Reader 1

You are a chosen race, a royal priesthood, a holy nation, God's own people – in order that you might proclaim the mighty acts of him who called you out of darkness into his wonderful light.

Reader 2

'We ask ourselves: Who am I to be brilliant, gorgeous, talented and fabulous? Actually who are you not to be? You are a child of God.'[4]

Leader

In the quiet, let us commit ourselves this Lent to becoming fully what God calls us to be.

Silence or music *1 min*

Leader

While some are called to very specific and difficult roles, *all* of us are called to love and support our Christian brothers and sisters.

Reader 1

Consider the claim of Scottish theologian William Barclay:

One of the highest of human duties is the duty of encouragement. It is easy to laugh at men's ideals; it is easy to pour cold water on their enthusiasm; it is easy to discourage others. The world is full of discouragers. We have a Christian duty to encourage one another. Many a time a word of praise or thanks or appreciation or cheer has kept a man on his feet. Blessed is the man who speaks such a word.[5]

Reader 2

Consider this quote from the twelfth-century monk Aelred:

No medicine is more valuable, none more efficacious, none better suited to the cure of all our temporal ills than a friend to whom we may turn for consolation in time of trouble – and with whom we may share our happiness in time of joy.[6]

Leader
In the silence, ask God to make you into a good friend and a good encourager. Ask God to remind you of someone known to you who is living out a tough calling. Then ask how you might best support them.

Silence or music   *1 min*

All
> *Dear Loving Lord*
> *We are only small people in a big and scary world.*
> *We stumble over our words and our actions,*
> *And often we fail to speak or act at all.*
> *We come now in trust*
>> *- that you can make strength out of our weakness,*
>> *- that you love us and you call us,*
>> *- and that you give us the friendship of your Holy Spirit.*
> *In that trust, we are willing to step out and speak up.*
> *Give us grace to be fully what you want us to be.*
> *Amen.*

TO TAKE IT FURTHER

Best actor in a supporting role

Therefore encourage one another and build each other up ....
(1 Thessalonians 5:11)

Read
1 Thessalonians 5:11-14

If like me you are a sucker for watching award ceremonies, like the BAFTAs or the Oscars, you will be familiar with the category for 'Best Actor in a Supporting Role.' I've been considering this and would like to suggest it as a category to be rewarded more often in real life.

The zeitgeist of our twenty-first-century western world is all about individuality, about self-fulfilment as our right – in fact, much more about rights than duties in general. Other generations would have been puzzled by this emphasis. They saw themselves as part of a whole: a family, a community, a nation – much more about *us* and much less about *me*. In many other cultures in the world people still do have this emphasis. I'm not about to call down evil on what has been called the 'me generation' – I'm part of it – but I do feel we rather set ourselves up to be disappointed.

Most of us never do get the chance to be centre stage. Most of us are destined to remain in the background: not a lead player but a supporting role, not the star of our own show, but a bit part in someone else's. And maybe we'd enjoy life better if we accepted that is how things are.

In fact, that's what draws me each year to waste time watching BAFTAs and Oscars. I won't deny I enjoy the posh frocks, the sardonic presenters, the blubbing 'I wanna thank my mom' speeches, but what I really like is when some unknown back-room boy or girl suddenly gets the honours. I love it when someone who's been quietly slaving away at something they believe in – sound design, animation, lighting – gets the applause. I also like to see those who facilitate, those who believe in other people's talent or work to make them look better or give them the words to say – the producers, the agents, the make-up artists – up there getting acknowledgement as well. I especially loved it when David Seidler, writer of *The King's Speech*, after a lifetime of slogging away at his craft, suddenly swept all the awards at the age of 73.

So let's hear it for the supporting role. Because if there is anything our society is in need of right now, I'd say it was a re-evaluation of the importance of support. How about if teachers in inner-city comprehensive schools and care workers with elderly dementia sufferers were honoured more than footballers and TV presenters? What if quietly building up those who've been brave enough to take on a leadership role was considered more of a sport than loudly knocking them down?

And while we're into radical rethinking, what if we did begin to major on duties rather than rights? William Barclay has claimed that:

> One of the highest of human duties is the duty of encouragement.[7]

What if we really believed that and sought to carry it out?

Lionel Logue's unfulfilled ambition was to be a leading actor. But what life gave him was a supporting role: patiently trying to unravel the damage done to shell-shocked soldiers and timid small boys – one of whom happened to become a king. And it turned out that this was much the higher part. As the film shows, it wasn't only the therapy itself. The creative methodology and technical skills he brought to it were important, but it was his gift of inspiring confidence, his capacity to be an encourager, his willingness to be a friend that really made the difference.

If you can, at this point take a few minutes for a simple exercise. Think for a moment of two or three people you have encountered in the last few days. What was that encounter like? What did you know of their circumstances or sense of their mood? Now rerun the encounter from their point of view. Did they see you as friendly, hostile or indifferent? Did they come away from the encounter feeling lighter or brighter, or did you add to the burdens of their day? Did you inspire their confidence or deflate it?

And how might God have viewed the encounter? Remember that is the only audience who really matters. It may be God's viewpoint that the poet William Wordsworth was thinking of when he wrote of:

> ... that best portion of a good man's life,
> his little, nameless, unremembered acts
> of kindness and of love.[8]

If so, when the divine review is written of our lives and times, these acts will not be unremembered.

Our world is hungry for friendship. It is full of those who yearn for appreciation, those who haven't received a smile today, haven't had anyone actually look in their eyes or listen to their words. It is full of those with anger waiting to be defused, with potential waiting to be unlocked, those who would blossom if only someone believed in them. It is full of those who are scarred by rejection, wearied by criticism, those who don't even know what it's like to be built up rather than constantly knocked down.

You may be one of those people yourself. If so, bear in mind that the best way to find a friend is to be one. And just in the doing of it there is blessing, because to be a friend is to take on the divine nature itself. So don't be afraid of playing a supporting role. Perhaps this is the highest role that any of us can ever play – simply that of being a friend.

Lord who walks with me on my journey,
Help me this day to notice those who need encouraging.

Teach me the skills of a supporter :
   the power of eye contact, of sharing a joke,
   of constructive criticism, of shared silence in the face of
      sorrow.
Teach me to say 'I'll pray for you' – and mean it.
Make me willing to 'waste' time on someone 'unimportant',
      To hang in with someone unpopular,
      To carry someone's burden a mile or two,
      To massage their bruised ego, or strengthen their weary
      arms.
Lord, I turn to you to show me, because you are master of it,
Divine encourager, encourage me, I pray.

WEEK 2

'I'm just saying you *could* be king.
You could do it!'

TO START YOU THINKING

Unafraid of fear

But Moses said, 'O Lord, please send someone else ....' (Exodus 4:13)

Read
Exodus 4:10-16

Interesting question: if Moses had refused the challenge to liberate his people from Egypt, would God have sent someone else?

Counterfactual histories are rather popular these days. What if Nelson had given in to his perpetual seasickness and decided a naval career was not for him? What if Hitler had been accepted by the Vienna Academy of Fine Arts instead of twice rejected? What if Edward VIII had been allowed a morganatic marriage with Mrs Simpson? What if Bertie had refused to take up the challenge of the British throne? Or taken it up, but failed to speak in public because it was such an impossible ordeal? Fascinating but frustrating questions to which we can never know the answers.

Certainly there could have been no one so uniquely placed as Moses to fulfil God's calling. A Jew who had actually been brought up in the Egyptian royal household, he had access to Pharaoh and could speak to him on his terms. An adopted Egyptian who had risked everything when he intervened to kill an oppressor, he had proved his commitment to justice and to his enslaved people. But by now Moses had found a new family and made a new life for himself in the hidden fastness of the Sinai mountains. There was no doubt that it was God who was calling – this conversation was taking place next to a burning bush after all. But Moses had run away once. Would he do so again?

Interesting that Moses' fear, like Bertie's, centred on his inability to speak: 'I have never been eloquent ... I am slow of speech and tongue.' With a bit of strange wizardry involving leprous hands and staffs turning into snakes, God had just proved that he would perform miracles on Moses' behalf, but even that was not enough. Moses knew that a great deal of persuasion and verbal authority would be needed in what he was being asked to do, and he knew he just didn't have it. In God's eyes that was not an obstacle: 'Now go; I will help you to speak and will teach you what to say.' Still Moses wavered. He simply didn't have the courage to go it alone. God, apparently a bit exasperated by then, pointed out that he didn't have to. It was all in hand. His brother Aaron was on his way, even as they spoke, ready to take the role of companion and act as his spokesperson.

I wonder if anyone who has been called to a challenging task has ever taken it up entirely without fear. I think I'd be a little worried if they had. I rather suspect that calling inevitably begins in fear and that it was always intended be so.

So perhaps we need not be so afraid of fear. If we wonder if God is calling us to do something, be it very small or very large, then the fear itself might just be an indication that we are on the right track.

It is, of course, the bravery to respond to the smaller challenges that prepares us for the larger ones. Moses may have been foolhardy in killing the Egyptian slave master, but he certainly demonstrated his courage and his willingness to put his head above the parapet for the sake of his suffering brethren.

Perhaps that too is a factor – compassion in smaller situations preparing us for empathy in larger ones. Certainly that was evident in the case of Lionel Logue, whose compassion for the tongue-tied young 'diggers' eventually gave him the ability to be of service to a king.

And as *The King's Speech* also shows us, it was Bertie's determination in overcoming his stammer (and perhaps Elizabeth's determination in finding the right help) long before the likelihood of him becoming king and certainly long before the threat of war, that made him able to meet the great challenge when it did come.

We all have dreams of what we would like to do in life. There is nothing wrong in dreaming dreams and nothing wrong in pursuing them. They may well be part of God's plan for us. But we have to be prepared for the possibility that what God wants of us is something else entirely. And it may be that what God wants of us is not one great big thing, but lots of rather small and insignificant things. Francis de Sales, a seventeenth-century French bishop put it this way:

> God requires a faithful fulfilment of the merest trifle given us to do, rather than the most ardent aspiration to things to which we are not called.[1]

I have been talking up to now about 'calling', but what Bertie took on in *The King's Speech* did not present itself that way, rather as an unavoidable duty. The word 'duty' seems out of fashion these days, and carries rather unattractive connotations. Calling has a nobility about it, it implies being special, being selected. Duty however speaks more of drudgery, imposition and lack of choice. I'm not sure however that the two are really so different. Most true callings involve a good deal more drudgery than glory – as many parish priests, poets and physicists would affirm. Most duties can be avoided – as countless abandoned elderly parents and fatherless children might testify.

For Dag Hammarskjold, the first Secretary General of the United Nations, it is the willingness to take on a duty that marks out someone with greater potential:

> To let oneself be bound by a duty from the moment you see it approaching is part of the integrity that alone justifies responsibility.[2]

To my mind duty is even more scary than calling. For me, the calling of writing brings with it the frequent fear of rejection slips and writer's block, but the duty of being carer to my elderly mother demands reserves of patience I constantly fear I do not have.

Still I rather suspect that in God's mind the two words are synonymous. What he wants us to do is what we ought to do. What we ought to do is what he wants us to do. A calling might yield more human glory than a duty, but in God's eyes it is the faithful fulfilling and not the end result that matters. In any case, he promises an ultimate glory far deeper and more satisfying that than fickle human acclaim. And in the meanwhile I'm beginning to discover a little bit of what Thomas Merton meant when he wrote:

> Duty does not have to be dull. Love can make it beautiful and fill it with life.[3]

Demanding Lord,
I am afraid of duties that seem unavoidable,
I am afraid of a calling that seems beyond my grasp.
I am afraid of risk, I am afraid of responsibility,
I am afraid that I don't have either the ability or the
stamina for the job.
Even so, Lord, I give you permission to drag me out of my
comfort zone.
I sign myself up to do both what I ought and what you want.
I might need a bit of help, Lord – you know that.
And so I trust you to supply it,
both divine strengthening inside and human
companionship alongside.
I trust it to turn up when I need it.
I trust you as God of both challenge and comfort.
Amen.

♔

SESSION 2

Chasing the dream or fulfilling the calling

Ask   *5 mins*
What were the main thoughts you brought away with you from
the last session or from the other course chapters so far?

Read   *1 min*
Ephesians 4:1

Brainstorm   *4 mins*
In popular terminology we often refer to some people as having
a 'calling'. List the sorts of jobs or activities that you would
classify as a calling.

Discuss   *5 mins*
What is the difference between a dream, an ambition and a
calling?

Ponder and share   *5 mins*
Does anyone here feel that they have, or have had a calling?
If so, what is it, and what makes you describe it in those terms?

Discuss   *5 mins*
So how do you think we can define a calling?
    Does it have to be a long-term thing?
    Do you have to have had some sort of external 'summons'?

Discuss   *4 mins*
How do you think you *receive* a calling?

Do you have to *feel* called or can it just be dumped on you?

Does it have to be something you *want* to do, or conversely is it more likely to be something you *don't* want?

In this session we explore three people who each find themselves with a calling that is maybe not what they would have chosen. Pay careful attention to this first clip, there will be some questions on it afterwards.

Show   *9 mins*
(Chapter 2) Elizabeth makes a visit, Logue auditions, Bertie tells a story.

Ask   *1 min*
When Lionel Logue tells his wife that he has an audition, what term does he use?

Ask   *2 mins*
Why do you think they put this audition scene in the film and what does it tell you about Logue?

Ask   *3 mins*
And what does the bedtime story scene tell you about Bertie?

Ask   *30 secs*
Did you notice what Bertie says when he comes in on Elizabeth finishing reading to the two princesses?

Ask   *30 secs*
And when Elizabeth explains to Logue that her husband can't evade his speaking duties and get another job, how does Logue ironically describe the husband's position and how does Elizabeth respond?

Ask   *30 secs*
Can you explain the term she uses?

We probably all have times when we feel trapped in a position we cannot escape, and we can probably all understand how Bertie yearns to fly away from his daunting responsibilities.

Ponder and share *4 mins*

What things in your life do you long to fly away from?

Ask *30 secs*

Do you remember the Shakespeare quotation that Logue uses when Elizabeth arrives at his consulting rooms?

Ask *30 secs*

Or in other words?

Ask *30 secs*

When Elizabeth goes to see Logue she is somewhat regal and condescending, though impeccably polite. But how does Logue describe her when he is trying to tell his wife about the visit?

Read *1 min*

Genesis 2:18 -25

Discuss *7 mins*

Just 75 years ago, the concept of a woman's role as being helper to her husband was a largely unquestioned assumption. These days it would be scorned as sexist. Do you think we should hang on to the principle of the marital 'helper' in this age of equality, and if so, how?

Ask *5 mins*

So in summary, what varied thoughts does this first film clip provoke about dreams, ambition and the nature of a calling?

In this next clip we jump forward to about three quarters of the way through the film.

Show *6 mins*

(Chapter 8) Abdication speech and Bertie's reaction.

In Edward VIII's abdication speech, he says :

> You must believe me when I tell you I have found it impossible to carry the heavy burden of responsibility and to discharge my duties as King as I would wish to do without the help and support of the woman I love.

Scriptwriter David Seidler has been quoted as saying that:

> The Prince of Wales' and Wallis Simpson's romance was not the greatest love story ever told, it was one of the most selfish.[4]

Discuss *4 mins*

From what you have seen in the film, or from what you know of history, what do you think? Could it have been right for David to give up duty for love, or was it a weak or selfish act of evading responsibility? Was it really impossible for him to have ruled without her help and support?

Discuss *2 mins*

Do you think that given Bertie's speech impediment, he would have been justified in refusing to take up the role of King?

At the end of that clip we saw Elizabeth trying to comfort Bertie, and telling him that she never wanted a royal life. In the original script, and possibly in the original film, there is a line that is cut out of the DVD version. In this she concludes by saying:

> 'But if I must be Queen, I intend to be a very good Queen. Queen to a very great King indeed. '[5]

Sarah Bradford, George VI's biographer says it was this that made all the difference: 'He married the perfect woman',[6] someone who supported him faithfully throughout his life. We also see in the film, just how important Logue was to him as a friend and supporter, right through his reign. Perhaps it is worth reminding ourselves that the Bible too shows that the role of helper is just as much a calling as the role of leader.

Read   *2 mins*
Exodus 4:27-31 – Moses and Aaron

Acts 13:1-3 – Paul and Barnabas

Discuss   *3 mins*
It may be possible to be a leader without a supporter or sidekick but is it advisable? What are the pros and cons of going it alone?

Brainstorm   *3 mins*
List as many functions as possible that a 'sidekick' can fulfil.

MEDITATION   *6 mins*

Leader
Bertie had lived in the shadow of a charming and confident older brother, adored by the public. In contrast, he was totally unprepared, and was arguably quite unsuited to the role. Yet history has clearly affirmed that he really was the best man for the job.

Reader 1
1 Corinthians 1:26-31

Leader
Bertie felt terrified and totally inadequate for the role. Yet he took it on. Despite his fears, he was willing to fulfil the calling he had been given. Have you ever felt out of your depth? Have you ever thought that God has called you to do something you simply can't manage? If so, according to St Paul, that could be evidence that you are exactly the right person at the right time. In a minute of quiet, ponder these

things and ask God to give you courage to serve him despite your weaknesses.

Silence or music   *1 min*

Leader

Many of us never get the chance to be centre stage. We seem called to be always in the background: not an actor but an encourager, not the star of our own show, but a bit part in someone else's.

Many of us do not get to choose the life we want. We are not called to the life we dreamed of. Rather, something we never wanted is thrust upon us.

But we always do have a choice. We can resent what life brings us, or we can welcome it as God's calling. We can try to evade it or decide to do it to the best of our ability. We always have a choice.

In another minute of quiet, ask God to give you determination to serve him in the circumstances in which you find yourself.

Silence or music   *1 min*

Reader 1

Ephesians 4:1-6

Leader

'I urge you to live a life worthy of the calling you have received.'

All

> *God of surprises, God of challenges,*
> *God of Eternity who sees the end as well as the beginning;*
> *Our life is not our own. It is yours, to do with as you will.*
> *We lay our lives before you now*
> *and ask you to help us live a life worthy of our calling,*
> *Help us to take our part in the body of Christ*
> *and to serve the Kingdom of God to the best of our ability.*
> *Amen.*

♔

TO TAKE IT FURTHER

The prince who forgot who he was

... that you may know ... the riches of his glorious inheritance
... and his incomparably great power ... (Ephesians 1:18 – 19)

Read
Ephesians 1: 2-19

Some years ago I was asked to write a drama sketch to illustrate
the opening chapter of Ephesians – not the easiest commission.
Faced with such a theologically heavy passage, I decided the
best thing was to be childlike, and so produced the following
little fable (adapted here from the narration to a mime). I don't
think it has much dramatic or literary merit, but when an old
friend asked for a copy a few months back, I realised it must at
least have had the virtue of sticking in her mind. It brought back
memories of the fun we had performing it and also reminded
me of how in writing it, I discovered a lesson I very much
needed to learn. And so, of course, when it came to writing
about royalty, it was now sticking in *my* mind and I wondered
if it might just be relevant.

There was once a prince ...
No, honestly, he really was a prince. I know he shuffled
around a bit, and stared at the ground and mumbled, and
always had egg stains on his shirt and often wore odd
socks, and I know about his strange habits of scuttling
away if someone tried to talk to him, and staying all day in
his bedroom with the blinds pulled down – but truly, he was
a prince.

The trouble with this prince was that he didn't really know who he was. Whether he didn't understand, or whether he had forgotten, or whether he was just too lazy to be bothered, I don't know. Perhaps you can decide.

His father, the King, had gone away for a while and left the prince in charge of the kingdom. He left with him his most precious royal scroll and his ring – the seal of his authority, the guarantee of all his inheritance and the promise of the father's return.

And he left the prince great riches – a magnificent treasure house of all kinds of wealth, and every bit of it available to be used.

He also left a mighty army – powerful, well-drilled and prepared for battle – vast forces ready to fight for the prince the moment he said the word.

But somehow the prince never got round to finding out what the scroll said, or using its authority. So when the people came to him and said: 'With all due respect, Sire, I don't think you've any right to govern this country', the prince said, 'Oh dear, no, I suppose I haven't. Perhaps you'd better take over.'

And when they said, 'Your father doesn't really care about what goes on here', the prince said, 'Oh dear, no, I suppose not.'

And I'm afraid the prince forgot all about the vast storehouses of wealth. So when the housekeeper came and said, 'It's the milkman, Sire, you owe him £3.45', I'm afraid the prince hid behind the curtains until he'd gone.

And when a frightfully nice lady came collecting for poor refugees, the prince said, 'Oh dear, I'm so sorry I can't help. Charity begins at home you know.'

And I think the idea of a battle frightened him a bit, because when a messenger came to him and said, 'Sire, Sire, the enemy is invading the country', the prince said, 'Oh dear, and we did put up those "Keep Out!" notices.'

And when quite soon the enemy actually came riding over the hill, the prince said, 'Oh well, we'd better pull up the drawbridge and stay safe inside. It's a shame about the kingdom, but never mind, eh?'

And so the prince who didn't know who he was, carried on living like a pauper and a weakling, while the kingdom slowly went to rack and ruin.

I don't know what the father said when he came back, but I don't think I would have liked to have been that son, would you?

The irony of *The King's Speech*, of course, is that it was Bertie's own father, the King himself, who had so undermined his confidence. George V was a father who really believed that making your children scared of you was a good thing. He had brought with him from a previous era the belief that barking orders or imposing harsh disciplines was the way to build character, and seemed vaguely puzzled that it hadn't worked.

Paul, in his letter to the Ephesians, wants to tell us that we have a Heavenly Father who is nothing like that. The opening chapter seems to be aimed at people with little confidence, and a glimpse at the circumstances of the letter's recipients explains why. Ephesus was a sophisticated cosmopolitan city and one can imagine that the fledgling church of new believers, dismissed as heretics by the Jewish community and scorned as religious weirdoes by the rest, might well have been feeling something of a beleaguered minority and were wondering what they had got themselves into.

Most of us feel lacking in confidence at some point in our lives. I was at a particularly low point when I wrote the story of the prince. I was a full-time mum, and though I refused to say that I was '*just* a housewife' when asked at parties, nevertheless I was feeling the '*just*'! Quite a few other factors had combined around then to make me feel something of a nonentity. Perhaps having a faith that seemed so at odds with the spirit of the age was one of them. Is there any believer who at one time or another doesn't feel uncertain and insecure?

I'm not sure there is any miracle cure for this confidence dip – sometimes the answer is just to plough through it – but it does help if we know who we are – ordinary human beings who have amazingly discovered a loving Father God. In the first chapter of Ephesians Paul seems desperate to get his readers to understand what this means and he is laying it on thick. He wants us to know that we are 'chosen', 'adopted as sons' , recipients of 'glorious grace... freely given' and of 'the riches of God's grace...lavished on us'. He wants us to open our eyes and see the 'riches of his glorious inheritance' and the 'incomparably great power' that are available to us.

Paradoxically, it seems that the breakthrough in confidence often comes only when we are able to acknowledge our full human weakness. It is then that we discover grace, riches and power that were waiting there for us all along.

In *The King's Speech* it was only when Bertie, warmed by friendship, could acknowledge his own humanness, that he was then able to fulfil his calling as a king.

> *Lord of lavish grace and gentle fatherhood,*
> *Come to us in our diffidence and distrust.*
> *Remind us of who we are,*
> *And give us a vision of who we could be.*
> *Help us to walk tall,*
> *Even when we feel small.*
> *Let no man or woman destroy our courage.*
> *Or rob us of our inheritance.*
> *Keep us from wasting our own potential.*
> *Or squandering our opportunities.*
> *We put our trust in you,*
> *And open our hands now to receive what you offer.*
> *Amen.*

WEEK 3

'You have such perseverance, Bertie,
you're the bravest person I know.'

TO START YOU THINKING

No short cuts

...like a man building a house, who dug down deep and laid the foundation on rock. (Luke 6:48)

Read
Luke 6:46-49

So then, what is your calling? Or put it another way: what are your duties, tasks or challenges right now? Or yet another way: what are the words from God that need to be translated into practice in your life? It might be good to take a moment and actually scribble a few answers down. Then put them aside until you have read the rest of this chapter.

Writing this in the run-up to an Olympic year, moreover a year when they will be held in my home city, means I am particularly aware of athletes in training. The news reports are full of them – young hopefuls with toned bodies and strained sinews, and not one of them – that I've read about anyway – is just sitting there waiting for it to happen. Every one of them is spending hours every single day in honing their skills, and further hours each day in maintaining their fitness. Each one of them is on a controlled diet, and working on ways to improve their motivation. All of them have put leisure aside and other activities on hold.

There is an oft-repeated story of Hokusai, a great Japanese painter and engraver of the nineteenth century.[1]

One day a great nobleman asked Hokusai for a painting of his favourite rooster. He agreed and told him to come back in a week. After a week the nobleman sent his servant to collect it, but Hokusai begged for a postponement. The servant came back two weeks later, then two months, then six months, and still the painting was not ready. After three years the nobleman was so angry that he came to see Hokusai for himself. Hokusai quickly took his brush and with a few elegant strokes drew the most exquisite painting of a rooster. That made the nobleman even angrier.

'Why did you keep me waiting for years,' he asked, 'if you can do it in so short a time?'

'You don't understand,' said Hokusai. 'Come with me.'

He took the nobleman into his studio. There all over the walls were endless drawings of roosters, the product of three years' work.

Out of that came the mastery.

Lionel Logue knew that if Bertie really wanted to master his stammer, it would be a long haul and would involve intensive training. There were no short cuts. Even when he was not going for therapy sessions, he needed to continue the training: mastering his breathing, exercising his jaw, making vowel sounds, reciting tongue-twisters. If he wanted to control this thing, it was an on-going and laborious process. Bertie believed it was important – though he didn't yet know how important – and so he was prepared for the long haul and willing to make the sacrifice.

Jesus was tough on his trainees. He didn't want anyone following him who wasn't prepared to take it extremely seriously. That is why he gave such an apparently unfeeling answer to the man who said he couldn't become a disciple until he had buried his father .[2] It probably wasn't as callous as it seemed – most likely what the man meant was waiting for his father to die, what could have been a period of years, rather than a literal funeral. It was also why Jesus made the comment that no one who had put his hand to the plough and then looked back was fit for the kingdom. And why he talked so much about denying yourself and taking up the cross daily, [3] of the foolishness of setting out to build a tower without working out the cost,[4] and of the importance of building on a firm foundation, even if it means digging down into solid rock to achieve it.

Why were the Olympic athletes working so hard? Why did Hokusai spend so long on his simple painting? Why did Bertie persevere with his speech therapy, and why did Jesus' disciples accede to his tough demands? Well, obviously because these things mattered so much to them.

So I suppose the first question to ask is: how much do these callings, duties, tasks, challenges or words from God matter to you? The next question obviously is: how much effort are you putting in to make yourself fit to fulfil them? And of course the answer to that question is in itself an indication of how much they matter.

As a writer, I've often come across people who say that 'God has given them' a story or a poem. Most often they assume that therefore all they need do is just write it down as it came into their brain. More often than not the end result is rubbish! Or at best a nugget of an idea that could have been infinitely better if they had learned their craft, worked it and polished it, subjected it to criticism and then worked at it again.

If God has given you a task, then he has given it for you to work at. There are no short cuts.

So the final questions are these: how could you fit yourself better for those things you feel are your callings and duties? How could you polish up your skills in order to fulfil them and how could you practice so as to make them seem effortless?

Lord of the long haul,
Sometimes I insult you with my half-hearted efforts to serve
you.
I apologise.
Sometimes I think I can take a short cut.
I am sorry for that.
Sometimes I refuse advice and often I get offended by
criticism.

Sorry, Lord, for my stubborn and weak-willed ways.
Help me to believe so much in what I am doing,
   That I do it to the very utmost of my ability.
Help me to concede that there might be room for
   improvement
   And help me to persevere.
Amen

SESSION 3

Pressing forward and breaking through

Ask   *4 mins*
What's the hardest thing you've ever had to learn to do?

Ask   *4 mins*
Did you achieve it? if so, what were the factors that helped you
achieve your goal?

Ask   *4 mins*
Have you ever attempted to achieve something that you gave
up on?
If so, what or who discouraged you?

Show   *5 mins*
(Chapter 4) Bertie begins training with Logue

Ask   *3 mins*
In this clip we see Bertie persevering but not as yet succeeding.
What are the factors that make him battle on?

Ponder and share   *7 mins*
If you were to use the imagery of travel to describe your life at
the moment, which metaphor might you use? A long walk, a
mountain climb, a gentle stroll, a ride of some sort, a thicket, a
jungle, a maze? All of us go through many different stages in
our life journey and there are no right or wrong answers here.
In a few moments of silence, think about this. If an image comes
to mind, however unlikely, then stick with it and see what it
might have to say to you.

In the original script, in the scene at the end of this clip Bertie is able to relax and continue the speech successfully, to Elizabeth's great relief. In the director's commentary, Tom Hooper explains that he decided it was too soon in the story to see Bertie overcoming his problems, so he cut it out.

Discuss   *4 mins*
Do you think the media feeds us with too many 'easy' success stories and happy endings – or maybe not enough of them? Either way, what sorts of programmes are the most guilty?

Discuss   *4 mins*
Do you think the Christian messages you hear focus too much on success and happy endings – or again, maybe not enough?

Read   *2 mins*
Philippians 3:12-14
Hebrews 12:1-3

Ask   *1 min*
What are the two metaphors for movement here and what are the two character traits expressed?

Read   *2 mins*
Romans 5: 1-5
James 1:2-4

Ask   *1 min*
What are the two things that call for perseverance in these passages?

Ask   *1 min*
And what are the outcomes?

Clearly as Christians perseverance is a vital characteristic that we all need. But sometimes despite the utmost perseverance we just don't seem to get the breakthrough we need. Let's look now at how Bertie breaks through to a new level.

As you watch the following clip, pay close attention. You're going to be questioned on what the characters say.

Show   8 *mins*
(Chapter 6) Bertie returns to see Logue after his father's death.

Brainstorm   5 *mins*
List as many things as you can that came out in that scene about Bertie's childhood and general background that might have contributed to his stammer.

It's interesting that the old King's last words did actually acknowledge the truth of those Bible verses we just read. He did come to realise that in Bertie suffering and struggle had indeed produced perseverance and character.

Ask   2 *mins*
But what reasons can you imagine that there might have been for him never telling Bertie that to his face?

Ask   5 *mins*
What do you think was Bertie's big breakthrough in that scene and at what point did it occur?

Ask   4 *mins*
Why do you think Logue was initially so insistent that the therapy should contain a personal element?

Let us return now to one of the readings we had last week.

Read   1 *min*
1 Corinthians 1:27-30

Discuss   5 *mins*
God has chosen the weak – but do you think it is possible to fulfil God's calling if we never admit to our weakness?

Discuss   *2 mins*

If revealing our personal lives and our vulnerability is necessary in order to move on, why do you think this might be?

MEDITATION   *8 mins*

Reader 1
Hebrews 4:12-16

Leader
The scary thing about the Christian faith is that God knows everything about us. Nothing is hidden. The wonderful thing about the Christian faith is that we have in Jesus a friend who not only understands the hidden things but sympathises with them. The difficult thing is sometimes to acknowledge these hidden things to ourselves.

Use the time of quiet now to 'speak' silently in your head any painful things that lie long buried.

In your mind's eye, 'approach the throne of grace' and lay them there. Receive in exchange, mercy and grace.

Silence of music   *1 min 30 secs*

Reader 2
Psalm 139:1-16, 23-24

Silence   *30 secs*

Leader
Let us return now to the imagery of that reading from Philippians where Paul talks about pressing on towards the goal. Return too to the idea of your life as a journey and the image of travel that describes your life at the moment.

In the following time of quiet, think about your main goal at the moment and how you might persevere in the journey from here to there.

Silence or music   *2 mins*

All
> *Lord, we are not honed athletes or eloquent speakers,*
> > *Rather we stumble and stammer towards our goals,*
> > > *Not even sure if we really want to reach them.*
> *Lord, we are not fit and strong.*
> > *Rather we are damaged goods,*
> > > *Weakened from the pummelling of the past.*
> *But Lord, we take courage in this:*
> *That God has chosen the weak things of the world to shame the strong.*
> *Lord, take us as we are and use us as you will.*
> *Give us perseverance and the drive to travel on.*
> *Amen.*

❦

TO TAKE IT FURTHER

The breakthrough moment

> Flesh gives birth to flesh, but the Spirit gives birth to spirit.
> (John 3:6)

Read
John 3:1-8

Bertie worked and worked at the technical tools to control his stammer, but it was not enough. Lionel Logue knew it would not be. Right from the start, when he tried to get Bertie to talk about his earliest memories, he knew that something deeper inside would need to be unlocked. Since Bertie would only come on his own terms: 'Strictly business. No personal nonsense', Logue agreed. He worked with what he had – and he waited. Gradually he gained Bertie's trust until the moment came when he would begin to unburden himself. It came after the old king's death – perhaps the first time when Bertie could even acknowledge to himself the depths of his childhood pain. That scene was a first in another profound way: the first time Bertie could allow himself to have a friend. 'What are friends for?' asks Logue. 'I wouldn't know,' answers Bertie.

I talked in the preceding chapter about the need for hard work and perseverance, but I knew as I did so, that it would not be quite enough. Whatever the task before you, sometimes all the hard work in the world simply can't carry you through. You may learn the craft, practice your skills, push yourself as hard as you can, strive and struggle, travail and toil – and still that indefinable spark is missing. It is at times like these that you acknowledge the wisdom of Thomas Edison's formula for genius: '99% perspiration and 1% inspiration.'[5]

But how can we find the inspiration and when does it occur?

As I thought about this, I was reminded of the episode in the gospel where Nicodemus comes to see Jesus by night. As a member of the Jewish ruling council, Nicodemus was one of the religious elite. To get to that position, he must have studied long and hard and laboured diligently to prove himself. Now he had got to the top, and you'd think that would have been enough. But the fact that he came so secretly to see Jesus, implies that it wasn't. Whatever Nicodemus' overt reason for the meeting, Jesus' strange response suggests that he sensed the need beneath.

This passage is very often used for its evangelistic potential: 'You must be born again', 'For God so loved the world ...' etc., and so the rather strange remark in verse 6 about flesh and spirit is often overlooked. I think it must be Jesus' version of perspiration versus inspiration. He is trying to tell Nicodemus that what his religious efforts produced were religious results. They would not result in the spiritual breakthrough he craved.

Whether Nicodemus found the spiritual new birth he needed is not recorded. His only other appearance in the gospel record is another secretive excursion, when after the death of Jesus, he went with Joseph of Arimathea to reclaim the body, taking costly perfumes with which to embalm it. The fact that he does not appear thereafter suggests that his spiritual yearnings remained hidden and unfulfilled. Perhaps he, like Bertie, would have 'None of this personal nonsense'. Perhaps he remained locked inside his public persona, unable to turn his back on his religious security and unable to break through.

Someone who did discover such a breakthrough, with powerful results, was John Wesley. Wesley was a determined and very religious young man. While studying in Oxford he became a founder member of something called the Holy Club. Its activities included religious exercises, studying mystical writers, visiting the poor and prisoners ,and fasting twice weekly. At that point he could have taken up a safe Anglican parish and continued in the same vein, but it was not enough.

He decided to respond to a call to go to the new American colony of Georgia to evangelise the primitive Indians. Wesley soon gave up his attempt with the Native Americans however, to work among the colonists themselves. Basically he made a big mess of it. It was all to do with courting a woman and then breaking it off. After her understandable fits of pique at his vacillations, he refused her communion. She and her new husband then indicted him for ecclesiastical irregularities. In the end he quit the colony – essentially a fugitive from justice. So much for holiness!

But it was in his contact with some humble and primitive Moravian believers that he glimpsed something deeper. He had shared the outward voyage to Georgia with some of them and been impressed by their calm in a terrifying storm. Back in London, he sought out one of their leaders and weary and ashamed went to him for counsel. It was soon after this at a Moravian meeting that the breakthrough occurred – the famous moment when he described himself as having been 'strangely warmed'. Quite what happened is hard to define – as all spiritual breakthroughs tend to be – but clearly 'the Spirit had given birth to spirit'. Wesley went on to be responsible for the Methodist revival, the greatest spiritual awakening in English history, one that transformed society and is credited by some historians as staving off the sort of bloody revolution that occurred in France.

The wind of the spirit, as Jesus said, 'blows wherever it pleases'. Breakthrough moments are elusive, be they the big one-off, life-changing ones or the small day-by-day, task-by-task ones. We cannot command them to appear. We can, however, put the right conditions in order. They seem to come only when we have reached the end of our own efforts, when we admit, at least to ourselves, our weakness and need. But very often the most genuine admission and therefore the real breakthrough is only when we reveal our need to someone else. We may need to say very little. Nicodemus's opening remarks were unspecific: 'We know you are a teacher who has come from God'. Bertie's breakthrough moment came, I think, with the simple admission: 'I'd kill for something stronger.' Good counsellors like Jesus or Lionel Logue can pick up the signals. More importantly, so can the counsellor that God has given within us – the Holy Spirit.

Nothing comes to us in life without effort, but inspiration – the breathing into us of the life of the Spirit – awaits the moment when we acknowledge that perspiration alone is not enough.

Lord of the long hard road,
I come to you weary
  And bring you my efforts.
How foolish I am, Lord,
  So often just struggling on,
    Refusing to open up the personal stuff,
    Refusing to reveal the roots of my weariness.
But now I am here
  And I breathe deeply
    Longing to inhale the fresh sweet air of your Spirit.
Come, Holy Spirit, inspire me now I pray.
Amen.

WEEK 4

'I was informed after the fact
my father's last words were
"Bertie has more guts than the
rest of his brothers put together."
Couldn't say that to my face.'

TO START YOU THINKING

The 'No Discouragement' rule

Out of the same mouth come praise and cursing. (James 3:10)

Read
James 3: 5-10

Did you know that according to William Barclay:

There is a regulation in the Royal Navy which says: 'No officer shall speak discouragingly to another officer in the discharge of his duties.'[1]

Now there's an interesting thought. Can you imagine if that rule was extended to other establishments? Can you imagine a family, a school, a workplace, a church where no one was ever put down, nobody's effort ever ignored, no one's questions dismissed as stupid, no one compared unfavourably to someone else, nobody subjected to sarcasm, damned by faint praise or made the butt of jokes? Can you imagine if the remark 'I can't believe you've gone and done that again!' were to be a punishable offence, if 'What a load of idiots' incurred an instant fine, if 'Oh, please!' was subject to a written warning and 'You really are rubbish' meant instant dismissal?

The apostle James describes the tongue as 'full of deadly poison'. There are many ways of spreading verbal poison: gossip, lies, incitement to hatred; but one of the worst is discouragement. It is particularly effective in young lives, as Bertie's story in *The King's Speech* shows. It may not be possible to prove that his stammer was provoked by his painful childhood, but the connection seems all too obvious.

Jesus reserved his strongest condemnation for those who destroy young lives:

> But if anyone causes one of these little ones who believe in me to sin, it would be better for him to have a millstone hung around his neck and to be drowned in the depths of the sea.[2]

And discouragement is one of the strongest causes of sin. It provokes frustration, confusion, anger, and pain that smoulder and eventually erupt in damage to others. James's image of the tongue as a spreading blaze is especially true of discouragement. It is those who feel the most insecurity and inadequacy themselves, however cleverly they hide it, who are quickest to criticise and put down others. It can spread from individuals through families, establishments, nations and even down through generations.

There is one obvious solution to the problem of the errant tongue: zip your lip, pipe down, shut up! This seems to be James' preferred choice. In chapter 1 verse 19, he advises that:

> Everyone should be quick to listen, slow to speak...

It's a brilliant piece of advice that all of us would do well to follow, but it is not the whole story. We all know the truth of another maxim:

> Evil triumphs when good men keep silent.[3]

James is right that the tongue needs to be kept under control, but biting it is not necessarily the answer. The rudder on the ship can be used to steer in the right direction as well as the wrong one, and a ship without anyone controlling the rudder will soon end up on the rocks. So there are times when encouraging or challenging words are vital to point people in the right direction and avoid the shipwreck of lives.

Have you noticed how much more susceptible you are to

discouragement than to encouragement? Well, perhaps you aren't, but I certainly am. It has been said that one criticism outweighs ten compliments, and I would say that proportion was about right. No matter how many nice things people say to me, it's the nasty ones that stick. Poison seems to work that way. And that's why we can't simply refrain from discouragement but need to actively work at encouragement. That's why Barclay makes the comment mentioned before that:

> One of the highest human duties is the duty of encouragement.[4]

Some people I know are natural encouragers. They are always delighted to see me. They always notice something attractive that I'm wearing. They often seem to be impressed with what I'm doing. And not surprisingly I blossom in their company.

Sadly, I'm not like that. I'm much quicker to notice the negative than the positive, more inclined to use my great wisdom in pointing out others' errors, more concerned to avoid obsequiousness than risk a compliment. (Actually, I don't know why. Do you know anyone who couldn't do with a little bit of flattery?) I'm also quite likely to be so preoccupied with my own thoughts that I simply don't notice things that deserve praising. My memory is so pathetic that I'll most likely forget nice things I meant to say. So for me, encouragement is definitely something I have to work at. It's a skill I've had to try and learn, something I need to persevere at.

I've said that these nice friends of mine are natural encouragers, but, of course, it may be that they've had to learn to do it too. They may be making it look easy, because in the past they've worked at it so hard. It may be that they've practised it over and over again for so long that it has become second nature.

I think it may also be that sometimes what I warm to is just a natural outgoing personality, very different from my own. Some people's encouragement looks different. It is quieter. It has more to do with empathy, with asking questions and paying attention to the answers, with shared humour and with the occasional challenge. Compliments are rarer, but all the more powerful when they do come. Lionel Logue's encouragement was in this latter category. And clearly it worked.

So I need to learn my own style of encouragement, one that's right and natural for me, but more importantly what is right for the person I'm engaging with at the time. And for that I need the prompting and insight that only the Holy Spirit can give me. And thankfully, when I ask for it, very often it is there. For the Holy Spirit is the greatest encourager of them all.

Lord of encouragement
Forgive me those discouragements I so easily mete out.
Forgive me the careless words that slip out unbidden,
    And the caustic or cruel ones that shamefully I often intend.
Lord, teach me how to be an encourager
    And show me who needs to be encouraged this day.
Help me to pay attention to those I take for granted,
    Alert me to those who might otherwise pass by unnoticed
        Remind me of thanks that should be given,
                    And interest that should be taken.
Give me grace to compliment those I would rather criticise,
    And the ability to speak less and listen more.
Amen.

SESSION 4

Poisonous words and profane responses

This session is all about bad language, including the sequence where Bertie lets out a stream of profanities. Brace yourselves if you don't like bad language – we're going to confront it head on. Even if you feel uncomfortable with this, please bear with it. As Christians we cannot bury our heads in the sand. We live in the real world and we are called to care for real hurting people, who sometimes use language that is less than pleasant. We're going to watch two excerpts from the film where people speak angrily and at the end discuss which is the most damaging.

Show   *4 mins*
(Chapter 3, 9 mins in) Bertie attends his father's Christmas broadcast

Ask   *3 mins*
How do you think the king would have recounted this episode to someone else later? How do you think he would have reported on what he said to Bertie?

Ask   *2 mins*
How would Bertie have perceived what he said?

Ask   *2 mins*
What attitude do you think the King displayed towards Bertie in that clip?

Ask   *2 mins*
Can you remember any of the actual words that King George

used to Bertie when he was trying to get him to speak into the microphone?

Ask *3 mins*

How did the King use those words, and how might Logue have used them?

Ponder and share *6 mins*

When you recount an argument, do you ever find yourselves using words like: 'All I said was...'? How often do you actually recount the *way* you said it?

Are you even actually aware of how you said it?

Read *1 min*

Matthew 12:34-37

Discuss *3 mins*

These are incredibly strong words from Jesus. Why do you think he puts such a strong emphasis on careless words – things that are essentially fleeting and often unintended?

Discuss *5 mins*

How can we become more responsible for the words we utter?

Brainstorm *4 mins*

You may well have heard of the old World War II poster 'Careless talk costs lives.' Think of as many ways as you can in which careless talk can actually damage other people's lives.

Ask *3 mins*

What was the damage done to Bertie in that scene?

The next scene takes place just after the old King has died. Bertie has spent time with his brother and realised how powerful Wallis Simpson's hold is over him and how unsuitable he is to be king.

Show *4 mins*

(Chapter 7) Bertie talks to Logue.

Discuss *3 mins*

How do you feel about Logue encouraging Bertie to use obscenities?

Discuss *4 mins*

What do you feel our attitude as Christians should be to bad language in real everyday life?

Ask *3 mins*

So what in fact *is* bad language – can we differentiate between different sorts of words and different sorts of usage?

Read *3 mins*

Exodus 20: 7
Matthew 5: 33-37
Ephesians 5:3-4

Ask *4 mins*

What are the different sorts of bad language that these passages prohibit, and why?

Ask *2 mins*

Where does the sort of language that Bertie was using fit in this spectrum?

Discuss *2 mins*

Why do you think that Logue did encourage Bertie to use obscenities?

Ask *1 min*

And did it have the desired effect?

Ask *1 min*

Near the end of that clip, Bertie says that he is afraid of Logue's 'poisonous words'. What do you think was so poisonous about what he said?

Ask   2 *mins*
Both the King and Logue were trying in different ways to suggest to Bertie that in view of his brother's behaviour he might have to take greater responsibility. What was the difference in the way they approached it?

Ask   2 *mins*
Bertie was unresponsive to either of them at this time. Why do you think this was?

It's worth remembering that when we try to affirm and encourage people, sometimes they just won't be in a place to receive it. However that doesn't mean we shouldn't try.

Discuss   5 *mins*
Of all the words that we heard in *both* those clips, which do you think were the most poisonous?

Ponder and share   6 *mins*
Does listening to the old King's impatience with his son, or Bertie's outburst of obscenities, bring back any bad memories of discouragement or anger expressed to you?

In the following reading, listen carefully to pick out what you think are key words that relate to what we have been discussing.

Read   1 *min*
Ephesians 4: 14-15; 25-29

Ask   2 *mins*
What do you think were the key phrases in that passage?

MEDITATION   6 *mins*

Leader

Think back over the last day, and then perhaps over the last week. Ask the Lord to show you when you have been encouraging in your speech and when you have been discouraging. Ask him to show you when you simply missed an opportunity to say something positive. And when you may have said something carelessly that had a negative effect.

Silence or music *2 mins*

Reader 1

'God is love. Whoever lives in love lives in God and God in him ... There is no fear in love. But perfect love drives out fear, because fear has to do with punishment. The man who fears is not made perfect in love. We love because he first loved us.'[5]

Leader

Logue says to Bertie, 'I'm trying to get you to realise you need not be governed by fear.' In another period of quiet, think about any areas in your life in which you are governed by fear. In the quiet, ask for God's love to enter by the Holy Spirit and cast out your fear. If God puts someone else in your mind who is governed by fear, then pray for them in the same way.

Silence or music *2 mins*

All

> *Lord, forgive us for when our words have been a discouragement to others*
> *Forgive us for our lack of words when encouragement was needed.*
> *Forgive us for when we allowed others to discourage us.*
> *Forgive us for when we have shrunk from what you have called us to do.*
> *Forgive us that we are unwilling to be fully that which we could be.*

Forgive us that we have forgotten that we are children of the
King.
Lord, encourage us now, we pray,
and help us to encourage one another.
In the name of Jesus Christ
Amen.

TO TAKE IT FURTHER

Letting it out

Get rid of all bitterness, rage and anger....(Ephesians 4:31)

Read
Ephesians 4:25-31

But how? Paul makes it sound easy, but we all know it isn't. How can you deal with feelings that are so uncontrollable and often so deep rooted?

The obvious answer is not to let them take root in the first place, and here Paul does have practical advice:

Do not let the sun go down while you are still angry.

It's one of the best rules for a successful marriage. It's not easy, but it is possible, especially if both partners commit to it from the start. Anger may not be quite straightforward to deal with though, when it comes to others.

What if there is no way of working it out with the other person and you just can't seem to shake it off? Here, to be quite honest, the Bible doesn't have many obvious and direct solutions. It has principles, and the most basic of them all: 'Love one another', means we are not at liberty to take out our feelings on others. And since we are commanded to love even our enemies, it means we can't even take it out on them. But we are responsible, says Paul, for getting rid of all this poison somehow. So what are we to do?

There are many ways of letting out the anger inside and we may each have to find our own technique. Buying a punch bag is effective – according to a teacher friend of mine who comes home from school and pretends it's the headmistress. For me, walking – fast and hard and as far as possible – works well. (It would be running, but I get out of breath.) I find driving a car very fast is also therapeutic, but possibly not great for other road users! Chocolate and alcohol , I find, are not good – they may be very comforting, but they tend to build up self-pity rather than release it.

But one of the obvious techniques is language. Tom Hooper, director of *The King's Speech* explains that he believed it was vital to include the scene with Bertie's bad language in the film, as it was such an essential part of the therapy.[6] For screenwriter David Seidler, it was a scene particularly close to his heart:

> The naughty F-word is not in the scene to shock, nor for prurient interest. It is there because it demonstrates an important aspect of stammer therapy that I learned from my own stutter, and which all speech therapists I've ever spoken to agree has validity.[7]

He goes on to explain how as a frustrated teenager, who couldn't even find the words to ask a girl out, he once got so angry that he said a naughty word:

> That flipped an internal switch... The stutter melted away.[8]

As anyone who has ever hit their thumb with a hammer will testify, saying a rude word sometimes does feel very therapeutic. So does mouthing off to a friend about someone else who has upset us. Does that mean then that these are OK Christian behaviours? In our reading from chapter 4, Paul says that we are not to 'let unwholesome talk come out of our mouths' (v29). Paul doesn't really define what this unwholesome talk is. And maybe that is a good thing, because it means that we need think seriously about it for ourselves.

Personally, I cannot find any biblical ban on using the occasional 'bodily function' word at a time of stress. Clearly, using the name of God or Jesus is a different matter – we are degrading the name of one we love. Equally clearly, as Paul goes on to say in chapter 5 verse 4, it is inappropriate for people who believe sex is a divinely-given expression of love, and who put high value on respect and restraint, to indulge in 'obscenity, foolish talk or coarse joking' . Gossip and slander are out (Romans 1:29-30), so if we do want to talk out our anger with a friend – and I do think this can be a very therapeutic and sensible thing to do – we need to first ensure that it is a friend who is absolutely committed to keeping it between four walls, and then ensure that what we say is actually truthful and not exaggerated or one-sided.

The other obvious thing to take into account when we think about our use of language is the cultural factor. What is not shocking to you may be very offensive to someone else. So I would suggest that if you want to vent your spleen with a bad word, the best thing to do is to make up your own. What do you think writers of gritty soap operas do before the nine o'clock watershed? I find 'Sugar' and 'Fishhooks' actually work quite well, and there's nothing wrong with good old-fashioned 'Bother!'

But when it comes to 'unwholesome talk', I can't help feeling that God finds my irritable whinging, my criticism of others behind their backs, my jokes at other's expense far more offensive than the odd expletive.

There are situations though, when expletives are not enough. It may be that your anger comes from a time in your life, your childhood, when you were unable to understand the frustration you were dealing with, a time when you couldn't answer back and just ended up converting your anger into guilt. Sometimes the bitterness becomes so deeply buried, its roots so tightly entangled with who you are, that you can't even identify what the source of your bad feelings is. What then?

'Bitterness, rage and anger' must be got rid of. Bottling them up is not an option. They will almost certainly find their way out – in irritability or sudden fury aimed at completely the wrong targets, in depression, or even in physical illness.

Hebrews 12 verse 15 says:

> See to it that no one misses the grace of God and that no bitter root grows up to cause trouble and defile many.

Sometimes digging away at the roots of bitterness is necessary. When they are very deep-seated then finding a wise counsellor or therapist may be the only answer. It is not weakness, but the sensible and courageous thing to do. But sometimes we can just allow God's grace to do its work without digging – rather like a systemic weed killer which when applied to the surface growth will work its way down to the roots and kill them off. God's grace is there for just such tenacious problems as these. Don't miss out by pretending the problem isn't there.

Lord of my messed-up humanity.
Help me not to disapprove of those whose pain I do not fully understand.
Help me to find solutions to my own anger that are both ethical and effective.
Help my language to be both wholesome and real.
At those times when it seems my anger cannot be shifted,
Teach me to turn to you as the Friend who understands.
Lord, I acknowledge there is bad stuff in me that is very deep rooted,
Come Lord and soak me in your grace.
Amen.

WEEK 5

'I have a right to be heard!'

'Heard as what?'

'A man. I have a voice!!'

✠

TO START YOU THINKING

Faith in our voice

'You must speak my words to them, whether they listen or fail to listen.' (Ezekiel 2:7)

Read
Ezekiel 2:1-7

As the letter of James reminded us, words are dangerous. But they are also the most marvellous gift, the thing that makes us different from the animals. George Bernard Shaw in his play *Pygmalion* puts into Professor Higgins' mouth an exasperated challenge:

Remember that you are a human being with a soul and the divine gift of articulate speech: that your native language is the language of Milton and the Bible; and don't sit there crooning like a bilious pigeon.[1]

This Lent course is called *Finding a Voice* with good reason. Because I think Christians, myself among them, seem to have lost their voice.

My failing, or the one I'm most aware of at the moment, is just in ordinary conversation, particularly in group settings, over meals or drinks. I'm quite prepared to let conversation drift where it will. I'm only too happy to let trivia prevail: reruns of conversations that have been had many times before, church gossip or bar stool politics or who I want to win *Strictly Come Dancing*. It has occurred to me recently that now and again I might actually steer the conversation, bring up something a bit more challenging or truthful or interesting or off-the-wall. That's just one minor 'bilious pigeon' tendency that I'm conscious of right now. I suspect there are rather more serious ones that I'd prefer not to think about at all.

Ezekiel was just one more among many Old Testament heroes whose first reaction to God's call was to be terrified. And with good reason. He was to go to people who were stubborn and rebellious, tell them a message they didn't want to hear and back it up with some very bizarre performance art. (See Ezekiel chapter 4.) Don't worry, says God to him in chapter 3 verses 8- 9, I'll toughen you up:

> 'I will make you as unyielding and hardened as they are. I will make your forehead like the hardest stone, harder than flint.'

If I was Ezekiel, that was the point at which I'd have cut and run. I don't like having to stand up and be counted. I don't want to be hardened up. I've got a nice comfortable quiet life, thank you very much, and I'd like to keep it that way.

Of course, I realise that if most Christians felt that way, then faith would soon be seen as unrealistic and unnecessary, God would be relegated to a dusty out-dated concept and our society would lose its moral compass and become greedy and selfish. Fortunately most Christians don't ....

Oh, actually, it seems they do.

We cannot pretend otherwise: traditional Christianity is in retreat in the UK. Here and there are pockets of young vibrant believers, mostly at the charismatic evangelical end of the spectrum, but statistically most congregations are shrinking while the average age rises. Very rarely in our media are bold, intelligent voices raised for the faith. Few Christians are out there making their voices heard and spearheading radically different ways of thinking. There needs to be a drastic change. We need to speak the words of God to our generation. We need to stand and be counted.

And now I've frightened you. You're probably thinking you'd rather change to another chapter. You'd rather read about God's love and gentle encouragement and not being afraid. Frankly, I'd rather write about it.

I know who you are, you people who attend Lent courses. You want to be good and decent and follow the Lord, but you're not the sort to go out and shout salvation on the high street. You're not about to start writing a controversial blog, or lie on your side for 40 days outside the Houses of Parliament to show them they need to repent of their sins. And neither am I. I know who you are, because I'm one of you.

So here's the good news. I think the odds that God wants to call any of us to be an Ezekiel right now, are exceedingly low. True, he calls us to grow and change and, no, we can't guarantee that he won't tip us out of our comfort zone and ask us to do something a bit difficult. But God calls us as we are, not as we aren't. He meets us where we are now and moves us on. He's not going to suddenly teleport us to a parallel universe where we are not equipped for survival.

And personally, I don't think our society is like Ezekiel's. I don't know how you see it, but I wouldn't characterise our nation as full of stubbornness and rebellion. What I see more than anything is spiritual confusion. I think we are in a time of major transition and that the church probably does need to be radically different – but no, I don't really know how. I don't fear that faith will die, because I know God as a reality and I know humans need God. And anyway, what happens next is God's business, not ours. We are not called to stand with our backs to the wall, defending the 39 Articles until Islam or materialism or relativism mow us down.

But we are called to stand. I do think God's call to Ezekiel: 'Oh, mortal, stand on your feet',[2] has some resonance for us. That's why I picked it. Surely we are called to get up off our backsides and do something? Surely we should not remain silent? There is so much out there that needs changing. There are so many things about which we need to speak.

I like that old-fashioned expression: 'Oh, mortal.' It reminds me that God knows exactly how frail and fallible I am – bound by my own physical and mental and emotional limitations. My calling is to do what I can and to speak what I believe. No more and no less.

When Bertie made his first wartime speech, there was no problem of people not listening. They were facing an unknown and terrifying future. They were fearful and confused and desperate for a voice to reassure them and lead them on. The voice they heard had authority. It inspired them. It did so because in that voice they heard humanity like their own. They heard the frailty and they sensed the fear that lay behind it, but they also heard courage. They heard someone who had risen to the challenge despite his weaknesses and that gave them hope that they might do so too.

When, as Christians, we struggle to find a voice to speak authentically to our world, that is the sort of voice we seek.

Lord who gave me the divine gift of speech
Help me to use it
And help me to use it well.
I know that I may not be clever or articulate
But I also know that those are not the things that matter
*   most to you.*
Help me to be bold and honest, simple and true.
Help me to stand up, with your Holy Spirit beside me,
Speaking the words you call me to say.
Amen

SESSION 5

Eloquence for evil and stammering for good

The title of this course is *Finding a Voice* and in this final session, we focus on the importance of having a voice for good in the midst of a sometimes evil world.

Show *11 mins*
(Chapter 9) The Coronation

To us, knowing what we do of Hitler now, it seems mystifying that so many ordinary people were taken in by him. And yet they were. Bertie's answer to Princess Elizabeth points out a scary truth: that it is sometimes possible to be so carried along by the way someone speaks that we never really analyse what they are actually saying.

Ask *2 mins*
Have you ever listened to someone speaking whose sheer eloquence persuaded you into something you later began to question?

Brainstorm *3 mins*
Eloquent voices are raised in every generation speaking things that are at best distractions or distortions and at worst downright evil. What are the voices in our generation that deliberately or inadvertently turn us away from what is true and right? Where might we hear them?

Ponder and share *3 mins*
Have you ever stood up and said you disagreed, in a situation

where everyone else seemed to be fully in agreement with something you thought was wrong? If so, what gave you the courage to do so?

Ask *2 mins*

In that clip, Bertie's despair at the task before him comes spilling out. He describes himself as a 'voiceless King' and 'Mad King George the Stammerer'. How did Logue deal with this outburst?

Ask *1 min*

What did Logue finally provoke Bertie into realising?

Ask *1 min*

How did Logue define his task with the shell-shocked First World War soldiers?

Discuss *5 mins*

Do you believe that you have a right to be heard? If so, do you have faith in your voice and what convinces you of it?

Ask *4 mins*

Assuming you do believe you have a right to be heard, do you think you exercise it as much as you could or should? If not, why not?

Ponder and share *4 mins*

Has it ever made a difference to you, and particularly to your courage, to know that a friend was listening?

We have seen some of the following film clip already in Session 1. However this time, rather than focussing on the importance of Logue's relationship with Bertie, we will concentrate on the words of the speech themselves, and on the context in which they were delivered.

Show *13 mins*

(Chapter 11) The King's wartime speech.

Discuss *4 mins*

What struck you most about the speech itself and the circumstances in which it was delivered?

Ask *5 mins*

Our generation hasn't faced anything like the same challenges as our grandparents. Do you think we have had it too easy – or does our era have its own challenges too? If so, what are they?

Brainstorm *5 mins*

What do you think are the challenges that might lie ahead for us or the generation coming up behind us?

We never know what we may have to face in the future, but we can be pretty sure that all of us will have to face challenges of some sort. We look now at two Bible readings from Jesus and from Paul on how to face the future.

Read *1 min*

Matthew 10:16-20, 26-34

Ask *2 mins*

Jesus warns his disciples of scary times ahead, yet tells them not to be afraid. What reasons does he give?

Read *1 min*

1 Thessalonians 5:1-12

Ask *1 min*

St Paul warns the early Christians that their peace and security may suddenly be destroyed. How does he say they are to be prepared?

Ask *3 mins*

Do you feel that we as Christians are prepared for tough times? In the light of these passages, what preparations do you feel you might need to take?

Ponder and share   *10 mins*

As you look back over this Lent course and the film we have been studying, what are the lessons that you personally will take away from it.

MEDITATION   *6 mins*

Leader

The purpose of this Lent course might be summed up in Logue's description of his work with the shell-shocked young soldiers:

> to give them faith in their voice and let them know that a friend was listening.

In the quiet ask God how you might go on to encourage others in the group or back in your churches. How might you be a listening friend? How might you encourage another to have faith in their own voice?

Silence or music   *1 min*

Reader 1

St Peter says:

> 'You are a chosen people, a royal priesthood, a holy nation, a people belonging to God, that you may declare the praises of him who called you out of darkness into his wonderful light.' [3]

Reader 2

Jesus says:

> 'You did not choose me, but I chose you to go and bear fruit – fruit that will last.'[4]

Leader

Bertie finally saw beyond his fear and his failure and understood:

I have a right to be heard. I have a voice!

In the quiet that follows, let these words echo in your mind. Ask God to show you when and how to speak up.

Silence or music *1 min*

Leader

Jesus promised his disciples that they need not go it alone.

Reader 1

'And I will ask the Father and he will give you another Counsellor to be with you for ever – the Spirit of truth. The world cannot accept him, because it neither sees him nor knows him. But you know him for he lives with you and will be in you... On that day you will realise that I am in my Father and you are in me and I am in you. [5]

Reader 1

But the Counsellor, the Holy Spirit whom the Father will send in my name, will teach you all things and will remind you of everything I have said to you. Peace I leave with you; my peace I give you. I do not give to you as the world gives. Do not let your hearts be troubled and do not be afraid [6]

Leader

In the quiet that follows, you might like to use the image of Logue, standing by Bertie as he speaks out, as a picture of the Holy Spirit at work in your life. The world outside has no idea of his presence, as he silently encourages, directs you onwards and lifts you when you stumble – this is how the Holy Spirit works, as the unseen friend at our side. And in this lies a remarkable peace.

Silence or music *1 min*

All

Come Holy Spirit, strengthen us we pray.
Give us the courage to speak out for good,
   in a world where voices for wrong are often more
     beguiling.
Help us to overcome our fear.
Help us to find the right words to say.
Help us to believe that we have a voice and that we have the
   right to be heard.
Help us to be strengtheners of those whose confidence is
   weak,
     and encouragers of those whose task is to be a public
      voice.
As we move forward from Lent to Easter,
   we commit ourselves once more
     to be faithful followers of our Lord Jesus Christ.
Amen.

TO TAKE IT FURTHER

A say in how the story ends

> Be strong and courageous. Do not be afraid. (Deuteronomy
> 31:6)

Read
Deuteronomy 31:6–8

David Seidler, the writer of *The King's Speech,* understood just
how much courage it took for Bertie to make that vital first
wartime speech. He knew what it was like as a stammerer to
'grow up feeling you have no voice' – and therefore that you
must be substandard. A stammer at that time was labelled as a
speech *defect,* and it was an era when 'defects' were hidden
away out of sight. Apart from one rather insensitive and
patronising mention of it in a radio speech by the Archbishop
of Canterbury, Bertie's stammer was never spoken of publicly
at the time or in subsequent biographies. Seidler points out
another example from the era, of President Franklin D
Roosevelt, who was always photographed sitting down and with
a rug over his lap, lest people should see his legs that had been
deformed by polio. Disabilities were embarrassing, a sign of
weakness – they implied you were a defective person.[7]

Thank God, attitudes to disability are more enlightened these
days. But perhaps we still have a way to go when it comes to
our emotional weaknesses. Come to think of it, 'weaknesses' is
the wrong word altogether. The real weakness lies with those
whose emotions are so deeply buried, that they think they have
none. To feel afraid is not a weakness, but an integral part of
being human. As C. S. Lewis points out:

The emotion of fear is in itself no sin. The act of cowardice is all that matters.[8]

When fear is allowed to rule our actions it can become profoundly disabling, but fear met head on and tackled with determination is actually an *enabler* – the very thing that builds up our strength.

I hope you've got the message by now, that God actually has a preference for weak people. When looking for those who make good servants – and therefore good leaders – weak people are the ones he chooses. But just in case it still hasn't quite sunk in, you may like to turn again to 1 Corinthians 1:26-31, with Paul's remarkable assertion that God has chosen:

...'the foolish', 'the weak', 'the lowly' and 'the despised'.

He goes on in Chapter 2 verse 5 to explain why:

...so that your faith might not rest on men's wisdom but on God's power.

People who believe they know it all are not much use as God's emissaries. People who think they've got it all sewn up can be positively dangerous when it comes to leadership.

The last frightened hero from the Old Testament that I've chosen to look at is Joshua. Perhaps on the day of this speech, as Moses authorised him as his successor, Joshua didn't feel so scared, rather elated and buoyed up with pride. But it would not always be so, as the veteran Moses knew only too well, so he repeats:

'Do not be afraid, do not be discouraged.'

Joshua was to discover plenty to discourage him as he fulfilled his calling, and as is so often the case, it came more from his own people than his enemies.

Thankfully, Joshua had had a good preparation. He had been Moses' assistant since his youth.[9] He had been up Mount Sinai[10] and later into the tabernacle,[11] following behind Moses when he went to speak with God. Later God had specifically told Moses that Joshua was to be his successor and commanded him to 'encourage and strengthen him'. [12]

We looked in Week 3 at the importance of training for the task for which you have been called, but here is another key principle: look for a role model and look for a mentor. I understand all too well that people such as these are not easy to find. Bertie had struggled unsuccessfully with at least eight speech therapists[13] until Elizabeth's perseverance eventually led him to Logue – and what a difference that made. So persevere in seeking out those who can teach you. Ask the Lord to point them out to you. When you do find them, don't necessarily bombard them with questions. Just take time to watch and listen. If necessary offer to drive them places, or do their filing, or carry their bags for them.

Perhaps you are older in years and further along the path and your calling now is to be a mentor. I don't mean necessarily in a formal or official capacity, but simply as an older brother or sister or perhaps even a parent figure. How tragic that Bertie's father was never able to communicate his pride and trust until it was too late. How wonderful that Logue was able to come alongside like the supportive older brother Bertie never had. Who are those in whom you see a spark that needs to be ignited, or a confidence that needs to be bolstered? Is there anyone who needs you to show them you believe in them?

Joshua needed courage because he had a role to fulfil. Part of the reason that we are able to stand before God today, knowing of his love and commitment to us, is because of big names like Joshua and thousands upon thousands of unknown people like him – decades, centuries and millennia ago – who faithfully fulfilled what God had called them to do. And now the continuity lies with us.

In March 2011, Barack Obama, in a historic speech in Westminster Hall in London, referred back to the Second World War and the core belief in human freedom and dignity that carried the Allies forward. He defined it in a striking phrase:

'...a conviction that we have a say in how this story ends'.[14]

It's a conviction I long for us believers to take up. Because we – us ordinary insignificant children of the living God– *are* the makers of the story. We are chosen for a purpose: to keep the flame of integrity alive, to encourage the discouraged and love the unloved, to tell of the amazing Lord we have discovered and point towards a better way.

We are not alone as we struggle to have our say in the great story of humanity. We have each other – and as this Lent course ends, I hope you will continue to support one another, both in prayer and in friendship. But above all we have the Holy Spirit of God himself at our side. Like Logue silently encouraging Bertie on, he will be unseen to the world outside. Often even we will not be able to define when and how he came. But we will know he has been there.

So take with you now the promise of Moses to Joshua:

'The Lord himself goes before you and will be with you; he will never leave you nor forsake you.'

Lord of the great unfolding story of humanity
Help me to believe that I have a say in how the story ends.
Help me to play my part –
  Whether big or small,
    Centre stage or behind the scenes,
      Praised or criticised or unnoticed.
Help me to find my voice -
  To speak up for the foolishness of faith
    To speak truth into half-truths and lies
      To speak out against evil and corruption

To speak encouragement into struggling souls
I give you now my fear
May it be transformed
  by courage, perseverance, and the support of others
    into a strength and love that points to you.
Amen.

✤

ADDITIONAL SESSION

Having your say

Many groups decide that, having finished a course like this, they would like to have a further session to round things off – maybe something more informal, centred around a meal of some sort. If so, here is a suggestion for something a little different, something that arises naturally from the course itself and presents a practical challenge as well as offering a little fun. I have offered three elements:

- A quiz – Who said what?
- A challenge – 'What I want to say is ....'
- A closing act of commitment

WHO SAID WHAT?

This would probably work best if rather than just getting people to match the quotation with the name, you take the time to download and print out from the internet an image of each person listed and post them up round the room. Then get people to go round in pairs to match the quote to the person and write down the name.

1. I know I have the body but of a weak and feeble woman; but I have the heart and stomach of a king.

2. I have a dream that one day this nation will rise up and live out the true meaning of its creed: We hold these truths to be self-evident that all men are created equal.

3. Let me assert my firm belief that the only thing we have to fear is fear itself.

4. I've developed a new philosophy. I only dread one day at a time.

5. Ask not what your country can do for you, ask what you can do for your country.

6. Am I afraid of high notes? Of course, I am afraid. What sane man is not?

7. I have nothing to offer but blood, toil, tears and sweat.

8. Why are you still afraid? Do you still have no faith?

9. We can only do the right as we see the right and commit our cause to God. If one and all we keep resolutely faithful to it, then, with God's help we shall prevail.

10. If you had felt yourself sufficient, it would have been a proof that you were not.

11. This is the source of our confidence – the knowledge that God calls on us to shape an uncertain destiny.

12. I stand before you filled with deep pride and joy: pride in the ordinary humble people of this country .... And joy that we can loudly proclaim from the rooftops – free at last!

Answers are on p. 115 – 116.

'WHAT I WANT TO SAY IS ....'

This exercise picks up on the course themes of finding a voice and overcoming fear by getting each course participant to decide on something they really want to say – and then to actually say it.

It needs to be announced and explained in the previous session, so that each member comes prepared to participate. Each contribution must be no less than one minute and no more than three in length. It could take any form: a letter, a prayer or a poem. It could be read, completely ad-libbed or spoken from notes.

It could be about anything, spiritual or secular:

- Sharing your faith and what it means to you
- Being honest about your doubts or difficulties, struggles or scars
- An issue you feel strongly about: assisted suicide, abolition of student loans, save the local marshland
- Encouragement to a group member or someone else you care about
- A thank you to someone present or absent.

The only rules for the speakers are that it must be something they really want to say.

The only rules for the listeners are that they must give it their full attention and express their appreciation. You may like to allow one or two questions or *positive* comments to be addressed to each speaker.

CLOSING ACT OF COMMITMENT

Leader
The purpose of Lent is as a time of strengthening in the lead-up to Easter, when traditionally Christians renewed their baptismal vows.

As we come to the end of this course, let us reaffirm our commitment to be followers of Jesus Christ, borrowing some of the words of the coronation vows.

The prayer book bidding to those who have been baptised as adults goes as follows:

And as for you who have now by baptism put on Christ, it is

your part and duty also, being made the children of God and of the light, by faith in Jesus Christ, to walk answerably to your Christian calling, and as becometh the children of light.

Are you willing to fulfil your calling as one of God's special people, however that call might manifest itself?

All
I am willing.

Leader
Will you seek to be an encourager of those whose confidence is low?

All
I solemnly promise so to do.

Leader
Will you speak out for all that is kind and just and true?

All
I will

Leader
And so, in the light of the friendship of the Holy Spirit and Christ's promise that we need not fear, let us reaffirm our commitment:

All
These things which I have herebefore promised, I will perform and keep. So help me God.

All
May the grace of our Lord Jesus Christ and the love of God and the fellowship of the Holy Spirit be with us all ever more. Amen.

Leader
Let us go in peace to love and serve the Lord. Amen.

LEADERS' NOTES

*'Forget everything else and say it to me.
Say it to me, as a friend.'*

ON BEING A GROUP LEADER

Thank you for being willing to take on this important role. I hope you will enjoy it.

Leadership in this context is not about dominating the group with your own thoughts, but about drawing out the thoughts of others. More important than sharing your own wisdom is allowing the group members to tease out wise answers amongst themselves.

So resist the urge to fill every silence and jump in at every pause. Or if you do feel the need, do so with another question, rather than your own message, opinion or advice. You are there to facilitate others; in fact, very specifically in the context of this course, to help them to find their own voice. Your task is to let them know that a friend is listening.

So perhaps now is the time to hone your listening skills. Here is a reminder of some useful techniques:

- If you are unsure of what someone is trying to say, reflect back what you thought you heard, preferably using different words without changing the meaning. If in doubt, ask a question to try and tease out the background behind a particular comment.
- Notice the attitudes and assumptions behind what someone is saying. Listen out especially for misconceptions or different shades of meaning they may have read into the questions. If necessary, when differences or assumptions

become apparent, try and tease out what experiences lie behind people's beliefs and opinions.

- Listen to the feelings involved, as well as a person's words. Be aware of body language and what it is saying. Listen carefully for what is *not* being said.

- If you sense deeper issues behind someone's words, then make a mental note. Try and find out afterwards if it is something that requires further prayer or counselling. It is not necessarily your business to provide this, and almost certainly it will not be appropriate then and there. However, it is your responsibility to ensure there is some follow-up if needed – though only, of course, if the person wishes and it is not an intrusion of their privacy.

- Try and ensure that each member of the group contributes and avoid it being dominated by just a few of the more vocal participants. Don't be afraid of addressing questions to quieter group members by name now and again, but only after they've had a while to settle in, and only with a fairly safe and innocuous question.

- If your group includes anyone who is particularly fond of the sound of their own voice, then you may have to resort to desperate measures, albeit casually and with good humour. Here are a couple of tried and tested techniques:

    Have a small item – a shell, a pebble, a toy mouse – and make a rule that only the person holding it can speak.
    Find some noise-making implement – a bell, a whistle, a hooter – and agree a maximum length for each contribution. Then appoint someone as time-keeper and noise-maker when the speaker's time is up. Don't take this on yourself, your job is still to listen.

Note: This section is addressed to 'Leaders' in the plural. There will of course be one person in overall charge of your group, but my experience is that it is sometimes an enriched experience if group members are delegated to lead a session. This will only work, however, if each of them is understands the importance of preparing properly for the session, and most importantly is also committed to being a listener.

ON ACCEPTING DIFFERENCE

It's important to recognise that people may be coming from very varied backgrounds in terms of their Christian experience and beliefs.

In an ecumenical group this is especially important, as it may include everything from wishy-washy liberals to happy-clappy fundamentalists. Those two descriptions you may have noticed were appalling stereotypes. I included them on purpose, to remind you that we do all arrive with preconceptions and prejudices about people who are different from ourselves. What these sessions, and especially you as a leader, are aiming to do is to break down these differences and concentrate on what we have in common, our humanity and our relationship with a God who is far above such narrow-mindedness.

Bear in mind too that even within one congregation, in these days of church as a consumer product, people will probably have arrived there by very different routes and via very different experiences of Christianity.

THE WAY THE GROUPS WORK

FILM CLIPS

Before the session starts, make sure that the disc is set up ready on the appropriate chapter in the menu. Please make sure you know the idiosyncrasies of your DVD player. If you leave the film on pause, ensure that the player will not automatically drop out of this after a short time and leave the TV to come crashing in!

With one exception, all clips do start at the beginning of a chapter. For the one that doesn't you will need to have found the right place and set it on 'pause' (or 'stop' if it restarts at where you stopped) before the session starts.

READINGS

One way to keep everything running smoothly is to write each biblical references on a post-it note and share them out to group members beforehand so that someone has each passage marked and ready to read out when needed.

QUESTIONS

Each group session has four basic types of questions, in order to create a bit of variety. Please take note of the differences and clarify them to participants as the course starts, with probably a reminder at the beginning of subsequent sessions. The variations are:

Ask

A straightforward question that may simply require a factual answer, drawing on the film or a Bible passage. If it leads to discussion, that is fine.

Brainstorm

Try and get as many quick-fire answers (just one word or phrase) as possible. It will help to have a large pad of drawing paper (A2 size is fine for a smallish group) and appoint someone scribe to write down the answers. Don't get into too much discussion on these questions.

Discuss

This is the point at which ideas and opinions can be batted back and forth.

Reflect and Share

These questions are intended to bring out experiences rather than opinions. Allow 30 seconds to 1 minute of silence first before inviting people to share their experience. Try and resist too much discussion, and certainly no advice giving, although if one person's sharing of their experience prompts someone else to share that's fine in moderation.

MEDITATION

Each session ends with a time of meditation for about 5-8 minutes. Each includes two short periods of quiet. I have given a suggested timing of one minute each, but you may well find that giving them two or three minutes is better, especially as the group progresses and becomes more comfortable with the quiet. You will be able to judge for yourself whether your group is more comfortable with music in the background or with silence. If you do use music, obviously it needs to be fairly gentle. I find some of the instrumental music of Margaret Rizza useful in this context. Have it in the player ready to go when needed – and *please* fade it out gently rather than crashing out at the end!

You will notice that I have labelled the contributors to this session as Leader and Readers 1 and 2. I suggest that it may be appropriate to ask different people in the group to take on the Leader and Readers parts for each session, and to prime them beforehand to do so.

SESSION I
THE STUFF OF NIGHTMARES AND THE POWER OF FRIENDSHIP

Introducing the course

Check whether everyone has had a chance to see the film. If not, try and arrange a chance for them to borrow a copy between sessions.

Take some time to explain – and more importantly, agree – the ground rules on p.12.

Explain the varying types of questions, and how the meditation will work.

Reinforce the idea that participants should make time to read the 'before' and 'after' sections each week. Ask if anyone has any thoughts or questions arising from the Introduction or the first section. If so, it might be better to make a note to return to it later during the session.

Getting to know one another

You will have to evaluate how well the group participants know each other, if at all, and therefore how long to spend on this. If introductions are needed, then one formula might be to go round the room asking each person to introduce themselves along the lines of:

> 'My name is ………. (and I'm from ……….) and how I would most like to grow in my spiritual life this Lent is ……….'

If group members are from different Church traditions, then it might be a good idea to discuss the different ways in which they see Lent, referring them back to the definition in the Introduction on p.7.

If there are any group members who are not committed Christians but just exploring the idea of faith, then ensure within the opening statement that they are welcomed, with something like:

> 'If there are any here who have not made a step of commitment to faith, but are just exploring what it might mean, then you have an important place here and your views are just as welcome as all others.'

Show

Chapter 1

IN: Beginning of film.

OUT: After he spits out marbles in mouth. 'Thank you, doctor, it's been most interesting.'

Brainstorm

Fears inside Bertie's head as he waits to take the podium?

- Fear of failure,
- Of going completely blank,
- Of being told off by his father or scorned by his brother,
- Of being laughed at,

- Of the sympathy of others,
- Of being a freak.

The director of *The King's Speech* says he considers Bertie's worst fear to be that he may be mad. His youngest brother Prince John had epilepsy, but was considered insane and hidden from public view.

Ask
Recurring nightmares?

As an interesting aside: the film has another scene that depicts something that is apparently very often cited as a dream or nightmare: the Queen turning up for tea. It might be interesting to see if anyone has ever had that one.

Ask
Things flagged up in the opening sequence that make the ordeal more terrifying for Bertie?

- His father and brother have successfully done this before him.
- He is not just addressing a vast gathering, but the whole world.
- It is an era when speaking correctly with perfect elocution is incredibly important.

Ask
Possible reasons for God choosing someone who 'cannot speak' to act as his spokeman?

- V5 God knows Jeremiah so thoroughly that he knows his potential.
- V9 God wants him to speak the words he gives, not rely on his own eloquence.

Ask
What are the two 'Do not's in that passage?

- Do not say, 'I am only....'
- Do not be afraid of them

Show
Chapter 11
IN: Doors open and Bertie walks in.
OUT: After '...with the same depth of feeling for each one of you, as if I were able to cross your threshold and speak to me yourself.'

Ask
What makes all the difference in helping Bertie rise to this challenge?

- He is conscious of his role as King and of the needs of those who listen.
- Logue: 'Say it to me as a friend.'

Ask
Besides Logue, who else stands with him at this time, and how do they encourage him?

- Elizabeth: 'I'm sure you'll be splendid.'
- Churchill: 'I too dread this apparatus.'

Ask
What did you notice on the faces of those ordinary people who were listening to the broadcast?

- Fear. In a fearful man taking courage and addressing the fears of others there is a powerful bond.

SESSION 2
CHASING THE DREAM OR FULFILLING THE CALLING

If you feel it necessary, take time to re-iterate the ground rules for the group

If any discussion matters have arisen from last week's session or from the reading matter then deal with them at the beginning or slot them in later.

Brainstorm
How you classify a calling.

Supplementary question: Does a calling have to be a caring profession?

Discuss
How you define a calling.

Ensure the group looks at the short-term 'mini-callings' as well as life callings.

Discuss
How you receive a calling.

Something you want or something you don't want – this may be an old-fashioned concept, but I've certainly come across the sort of Christian teaching in the past that suggests it's not a 'genuine' calling unless it really goes against the grain of what you want!

Show   9mins
Chapter 2
IN: Elizabeth arrives at Logue's consulting room.
OUT: End of audition scene, after '*And a little more regal*'.

Ask
Logue tells his wife about the audition:
   'Oh, and I had a call.'

Ask

Bertie says to Elizabeth when reading:

'Oh, to fly away. Weren't they lucky?'

NB: The book, according to the script, is *Peter Pan*.

Ask

How Logue ironically describes the husband's position and how Elizabeth responds:

'Indentured servitude?'

'Something of that nature.'

Ask

Can you explain the term?

Indentured = legally bound, *servitude* = a state of slavery.

Ask

Shakespeare quotation that Logue uses when Elizabeth arrives:

'Poor and content is rich and rich enough.'

In other words: However much you do or don't have, if you have contentment you are rich indeed.

Ask

How Logue describes Elizabeth to his wife:

'Just a woman looking to help her husband.'

Discuss

Woman's role as helper

Don't let the discussion range for too long on the subject of women's roles, unless you feel it is really something that needs airing for someone. Note that the question is about the role of 'marital helper'- i.e. it could be the man supporting the women. Make sure it is clear that being a 'helper' or supporter is not necessarily a subordinate role.

Show   *6 mins*

Chapter 8

IN: Wide shot of David at desk. Just before: 'Until now....'

OUT: On visuals of posters 'God save the King', after '...he stammers so beautifully, they'll leave us alone.'

You might like to point out that the 'Stand by the King' and 'God save the King' posters at the end of the clip were part of a real life popular campaign to keep David.

SESSION 3
PRESSING FORWARD AND BREAKING THROUGH

Show   *5 mins*
Chapter 4
IN: Bertie lying down listening to gramophone
OUT: After 'Father, Father, Father', on car driving across field

Ask
What are the factors that make Bertie battle on?

- He knows how desperately he needs to overcome his difficulties
- He discovers that it is possible
- Elizabeth encourages him
- Logue is strict but makes it fun and not humiliating.
- Logue joins in with him

Ask
Media success stories or otherwise?

I was thinking of the many aspirational reality TV series: *Grand Designs*, *Build a New Life in the Country* etc. – where people always seem to triumph over the odds by the end. Makeover programmes and some cooking programmes, e.g.: *60 Minute Makeover*, *Ready Steady Cook* suffer from the same unreality: the decorating is always completed and the meal always ready in time.

Conversely, news and current affairs reports are almost always cynical about politicians and leadership and rarely credit them with a job well done.

Ask

Do Christian messages focus too much on success and happy endings – or not enough?

This may depend on the churchmanship of participants. At the more evangelical end, there is certainly a wealth of Christian publishing: biography and advice manuals etc., about how to be successful in the Christian life – participants may even have encountered the doctrine of 'prosperity gospel'. Alternatively they may come from backgrounds so hidebound that a successful church or dynamic Christian living are not even considered possibilities!

Ask

	Philippians 3:12-14,	Hebrews 12:1-3
Metaphors:	*Heading towards a goal*	*Running a race*
Character traits:	*Striving*	*Perseverance*

Ask

	Romans 5: 1-5	James 1:2-4
Calling for perseverance:	*Suffering*	*Trials*
Outcomes:	*Character and hope*	*Maturity*

Show   8 mins
Chapter 6
IN : Door opens. 'Bertie, they told me not to expect you.'
OUT: After 'What are friends for?' 'I wouldn't know.'

Brainstorm

- Things that came out about Bertie's childhood:
- Father never said anything encouraging

- Wouldn't allow Bertie to follow his own interests
- Teasing from David
- 'Get it out, boy.'
- 'I was afraid of my father and my children are damn well going to be afraid of me'
- Forced to use right hand
- Corrections for knock knees
- Only close people were nannies – but one was very cruel
- Johnnie – fear of being different, it wasn't catching
- He doesn't know anything of friendship.

Ask

Bertie's big breakthrough and the point when it occurred?
Clue: Think back to earlier meetings with Logue and what Logue suggested, that Bertie refused to do:

- Willingness to be vulnerable
- Willingness to reveal himself
- Willingness to confront those things in his life that he'd rather keep buried deep.

SESSION 4
POISONOUS WORDS AND PROFANE RESPONSES

Given the immense popularity of this film, I think we can assume that most people don't find Bertie's stream of profanities particularly upsetting. Nevertheless, this is a difficult issue for some Christians and you may find some participants who find it difficult to discuss – hence the introduction at the start of the session.

If you do encounter anyone who is difficult about this, try and ascertain whether bad language carries with it any painful personal connotations, or whether it is just over-prim cultural conditioning. The last 'Ponder and Share' question is aimed at rooting this out. If necessary, you could consider bringing that question forward.

It may be helpful to read out the passage on p. 74 (Week 4: To take it further) about the screenwriter's intentions and his own experience – but preferably not until discussion on the subject has got under way.

Show
Chapter 3, then fast forward to 26mins 30secs.
IN: Bertie making recording of his voice, before 'Hopeless, Hopeless'.
OUT: Bertie listens to recording of his speech, Elizabeth enters. Out after 'Hopeless, hopeless.'

NB: Apologies that finding the 'in' point is not easy, but starting at the beginning of Chapter 3 means about 10 minutes of unnecessary repetition.

Don't take time during the session to find the right place. Rather, just before the session starts, find Chapter 3 and fast forward to the 'In' point. Then press the pause button. You may prefer to then turn off the TV rather than having the image on screen.

Beware, however – don't do this too far beforehand as some DVD players will drop out of 'Pause' mode after a few minutes. Take time to find out your player's idiosyncrasies beforehand!

Ask
How would the king have recounted this episode:
Most of us in retelling an argument, try to justify what we said, and above all, to minimise the way in which we said things.

Ask
How Bertie would have perceived what he said:
Most of us in recalling criticism, place the most negative slant on it. If there is the slightest hint of impatience or unkindness in the words we will undoubtedly pick it up.

Ask

What attitude did the King display towards Bertie:
Bertie had obviously absorbed the idea that he was 'Hopeless'
many times before. This meeting just confirmed it.

Ask

Actual words the king used to Bertie:

- 'Have a go yourself'
- 'Get it out, boy!'
- 'Take your time – form your words carefully.'
- 'Relax.'
- 'Just try it.'
- 'Do it.'

Show

Chapter 7
IN: Bertie behind curtain at party. Just before: 'All that work
down the drain.'
OUT: In the park: after: 'These sessions are over.' They part in
anger

Ask

	Different sorts of bad language	Reasons
Exodus 20: 7	Blasphemy – using Lord's name it	God will not the excuse
Mat 5:33-37	Swearing – in context of making vows	Honesty obligatory at all times
Eph 5:3-4	Obscene and vulgar talk	Out of place for Christians

Ask

Where the sort of language that Bertie used fits in this spectrum:
It could possibly be said to fit under the Ephesians passage – but

dig a little deeper. Paul is talking within the context of sexual immorality and greediness. He is tilting at 'silly' talk, not angry talk. It seems to me that the sort of thing Paul is concerned about here is salacious, titillating or degrading conversation- which of course, can be conducted without recourse to any rude words at all.

Feel free to do your own trawl through the Bible but I am not aware of anywhere where it specifically talks about using obscene words to express anger.

Ask

Why Logue encouraged Bertie to use obscenities:
It may be worthwhile here to quote David Seidler's reasons for including them. You will find them on p. 74.

Ask

What were Logue's 'poisonous words'

- Suggesting that Bertie's place may be on the throne

Ask

Differences in the way the old King and Logue tried to get Bertie to see he might have to take more responsibility:

- The King says 'Who'll stand between us and the jackboots and the proletarian abyss? *You?*'
- Logue says: 'If you had to, you could outshine David ... You could do it.'

Ask

Ephesians 4:14-15; 25-29
Key phrases: you and members of the group may well pick out others, but these are mine:

- V15 Speaking the truth in love
- V 26 Be angry but do not sin
- V26 Do not let the sun go down on your anger
- V29 Only what is useful for building up

SESSION 5
ELOQUENCE FOR EVIL AND STAMMERING FOR GOOD

If you have decided to do the additional session then you will need to explain the challenge and do any necessary planning tonight.

Show
Chapter 9

IN: Bertie enters Westminster Abbey

OUT: After 'He appears to be saying it rather well.' Hold till end of newsreel of Hitler and end on Bertie's face staring. Cut at voice saying 'Sir'.

Ask
The persuasive power of eloquence:

Don't let this question focus only on politicians. It could be anyone, including Christian leaders!

Brainstorm
Voices in our generation that turn us away from truth:

- Materialism – advertising
- Atheism – scientific opinion presented as fact
- Cynicism – news reporting, gossip
- Scorn for religion – not always overt, often just an assumption that religion is irrelevant or only for the naive.

Ask
How Logue dealt with Bertie's desperate outburst:
Indirectly, by provoking him to anger, knowing that this would prove he could speak.

Ask
What Logue final provoked Bertie into realising:

- 'I have a right to be heard!'
- 'Heard as what?'
- 'A man! I have a voice.'

Ask

How Logue defined his task with the shell-shocked soldiers:

'My job was to give them faith in their voice and let them know that a friend was listening.'

Show

Chapter 11

IN: Bertie begins walk towards broadcast.

OUT: Royal family on balcony.

NB: If you need to make it shorter, you could spool through to the point at which Bertie begins the speech.

Discuss

What struck most about speech and its circumstances:

Try and draw out the circumstances: 'For the second time in the lifetime of most of us, we are at war.'

Ask

In Matthew, reasons why Jesus tells his disciples not to be afraid:

- V19 What you are to say will be given to you
- V26 Evil will eventually be uncovered
- V28 More reason to fear God and your eternal status, than those who can kill the body
- V29-31 You are of value to God. Nothing can happen to you without his knowledge.

Ask

In Thessalonians, how Paul says early Christians should be prepared:

- V6 Stay awake and be sober or Be alert and self-controlled
- V8 Put on the breastplate of faith and love and for a helmet the hope of salvation
- V11 Encourage one another and build each other up.

Supplementary question about verse 8:

What parts of the body does this armour protect?

The breastplate protects the heart – or the emotions, the helmet protects the head – or the intellect.

Ponder and share

Lessons from the course as a whole.

It might be worth going back over the headings of each weekly session as a reminder.

MEDITATION

The Bible readings from John are printed out from the NIV version, because they use the word 'Counsellor' for the Holy Spirit. Other versions use the word 'Helper' or perhaps less useful in this context, 'Advocate'. If group participants use different Bible versions it might be worth flagging up this difference before the meditation starts.

ADDITIONAL SESSION

QUIZ ANSWERS

A: John F Kennedy
B: Nelson Mandela
C: Martin Luther King
D: Aslan
E: George VI
F: Franklin D Roosevelt
G: Elizabeth I
H: Barack Obama
I: Jesus
J: Charlie Brown (Peanuts)

K: Pavarotti
L: Winston Churchill

1:G, 2:C, 3:F, 4: J, 5: A, 6: K, 7: L, 8: I, 9: E, 10: D, 11: H, 12: B

♔
REFERENCES

All bible quotes are from the *New International Version* unless otherwise stated.

Introduction
1 1 Peter 2:9.
2 Ephesians 1: 18-19.
3 David Seidler, '*How the naughty word cured the King's stutter'*, Mail Online, 20 December 2010.
4 David Seidler, quoted in '*The pillaged voice'*, *Newsweek*, 11 November 2010.
5 David Seidler '*How the naughty word cured the King's stutter'*, Mail Online, 20 December 2010.
6 Ibid.
7 C.S. Lewis, *Letters of C.S. Lewis*, 21 Dec 1941.

Week 1
1 Nicolas Berdyaev, *Towards a New Epoch*, 1949.
2 1 John 4:18.
3 John Gunstone, *The Lord is our Healer,* 1986.
4 Marianne Williamson , *A Return to Love*, 1994. (Erroneously attributed by many sources, and in previous Lent course *The Power of Small Choices*, to Nelson Mandela's inaugural speech.)
5 William Barclay, *The Letter to the Hebrews*, 1955.
6 Aeldred of Rievaulx, *On Spiritual Friendship*, 1167.
7 William Barclay, *The Letter to the Hebrews,* 1955.
8 William Wordsworth, 'Lines composed above Tintern Abbey', 1798

Week 2

1 Francis de Sales, *Lion Christian Quotation Selection,* seventeenth century.
2 Dag Hammarskjold, ibid, twentieth century.
3 Thomas Merton, *The Sign of Jonas,* 1953.
4 David Seidler, '*How the naughty word cured the King's stutter*', Mail Online, 20 December 2010.
5 David Seidler, *The King's Speech,* 2010
Screenplay can be found on http://twcawards.com/assets/downloads/pdf/the-kings-speech1.pdf.
6 Sarah Bradford, on TV programme *The Real Kings Speech,* 2011.

Week 3

1 quoted by Hans Rookmaker, *Art needs no justification*, 1978.
2 Luke 9:59-62.
3 Luke 9:23.
4 Luke 14:28-29.
5 Thomas Edison, quoted in *Harpers Monthly Magazine*, 1902.

Week 4

1 William Barclay, *The Letter to the Hebrews*, 1955.
2 Matthew 18:6.
3 Attributed to Edmund Burke, Source unknown, 18th C
Adapted from: 'The only thing that is necessary for evil to triumph is when good men do nothing.'
4 William Barclay, ibid.
5 1 John 4: 16, 18-19.
6 Tom Hooper, Director's commentary on DVD, 2010.
7 David Seidler, *How the naughty word cured the King's stutter*', Mail Online, 20 December 2010.

Week 5

1 GB Shaw, *Pygmalion* Act 1, 1916.
2 Ezekiel 2:1, *New Revised Standard Version,* 1989.
3 1 Peter 2:9.
4 John 15: 16.

5 John 14:16-20.

6 John 14:26-27.

7 David Seidler, '*How the naughty word cured the King's stutter*', Mail Online, 20 December 2010.

8 C.S. Lewis, *The Screwtape Letters,* 1942.

9 Numbers 11:28.

10 Exodus 24:13.

11 Exodus 33:11.

12 Deuteronomy 3:28.

13 Christopher Warwick on the TV programme *The Real Kings Speech*, 2011.

14 Barack Obama, speech in Westminster Hall, 25 May 2011.